HOLOGRAPHIC
GOLF

HOLOGRAPHIC
GOLF

UNITING THE MIND AND
BODY TO IMPROVE YOUR GAME

LARRY MILLER

HarperCollins*Publishers*

HarperCollins books may be purchased for educational, business, or sales promotional use. For information, please write: Special Markets Department, HarperCollins Publishers, Inc., 10 East 53rd Street, New York, NY 10022.

Drawings by Flip Amato

Designed by George J. Mckeon

Library of Congress Cataloging-in-Publication Data

Miller, Larry, 1947–
    Holographic golf : uniting the mind and body to
improve your game / by Larry Miller.
        p.   cm.
    Includes bibliographical references.
    ISBN 0-06-017006-9
    1. Golf—Psychological aspects. I. Title.
GV979.P75M55   1993
796.352'01—dc2093-15851   93-15851

93 94 95 96 97 ❖/RRD 10 9 8 7 6 5 4 3 2 1

Contents

CONTENTS

Acknowledgments

EVERY BOOK BEGINS with ideas, and for a book to become a reality those ideas must be regarded as being worthy of development by persons other than the author.

I want to thank Larry Ashmead of Harper-Collins for believing my ideas to be worthy, and for paving the way for the book to become a reality. Special thanks go to Scott Waxman, my editor at HarperCollins, for his professional, intelligent, and sensitive editing. Scott greatly enhanced this work with his technical competence and his creativity.

I wish to thank Dale McLarty of Katy, Texas, for her talents on the computer. Deadlines were met because of her efforts.

In 1992, my students at Glenwoodie Country Club in Chicago were unaware that they were living proof of the effectiveness of my developing teaching methods. I thank all of them, especially Bogey. Frank Jemsek, the President of Jemsek Golf (the family that owns and operates Cog Hill, home of the Western Open, and several other outstanding Chicago area golf courses) is a long time friend who has been very supportive of me in many ways. Frank provided me with the teaching venue where *Holographic Golf* was hammered out—on the lesson tee at Glenwoodie C.C. Manager Jim Mattas and his entire staff were extremely helpful and a pleasure to work with. I am forever grateful to Frank and his entire "family" for their friendship and support.

Judy Bailey, a close personal friend and accomplished amateur player, provided the two catalysts—the books *Golf in the Kingdom* and *The Holographic Universe*—which led to the formation of my ideas and ultimately this book. Her insights and suggestions were a great assist. Without her, this book would not exist. A very special thanks.

My parents, John and Peggy Miller, have been unconditionally supportive of my career (and personal life) since day one. My Dad taught me good communication skills at a young age, and more important, taught me patience and compassion, two qualities he personifies with dignity. He also introduced me to golf as a young boy, and encouraged me every step of the way. My Mom is the kind of person you want to go to war with. She has never run when the going was tough. I don't think I have ever heard my mother say no to anyone, for any reason. I owe them both in so many ways.

My three sons, Ryan, Jeffrey, and Jonathan, are the lights of my life. They are a constant source of pride and inspiration. My time with them has suffered during the writing of this book, but they are always in my thoughts and I hope they know how much I love them. And I thank their mother, Linda, for doing a wonderful job raising them.

My sister, Jonnie LaHatte, and her husband, Joe, have always been there as true friends and I'm grateful to them for a lot.

On a very personal level I want to acknowledge someone who is very special to me—someone whose influence will hopefully take hold and continue to enrich my development as a person. Julie Baudier makes the world happier and if everyone were like her the world would truly be a better place. To Julie Baudier and Puffy—I love you both.

And now, finally, I come to the one person most responsible for the successful completion of this book. Despite her threats to physically harm me if I embarrass her in print, I feel compelled to risk life and limb, all in the name of truth. The truth is, from the moment I conceived this book, she began to accumulate "titles." The duties she assumed are far-reaching and all-encompassing. Titles such as unofficial editor, agent, manager, sounding board, advisor, critic, secretary, psychologist—they all fit. Her loyal support and constantly fertile imagination were critical to my efforts. When the book stalled, she gave it more fuel. When it ran recklessly she calmed it. But most of all, her friendship and love never wavered, and so, because she deserves it, I'll go ahead and say that much of this book is for Connie Bousquet. (Despite the endless hours she gave in assisting me with this book, Connie found time to become the new 1993 New Orleans Country Club Ladies' Club Champion.)

Preface

IN THE MOVIE *Star Wars*, Luke Skywalker's adventure begins when a beam of light shoots out of the robot R2-D2 and projects a miniature three-dimensional image of Princess Leia. Luke watches spellbound as the ghostly sculpture of light begs for someone named Ben [Obi-wan] Kenobi to come to her assistance. The image is a hologram, a three-dimensional picture made with the aid of a laser, and the technological magic required to make such images is remarkable. But what is even more astounding is that some scientists are beginning to believe that the universe itself is a kind of giant hologram, a splendidly detailed illusion no more or less real than the image of Princess Leia that starts Luke on his quest.

Put another way, there is evidence to suggest that our world and everything in it are only ghostly images, projections from a level of reality so beyond our own that it is literally beyond both space and time.

The main architects of this astonishing idea are two of the world's most eminent thinkers: University of London physicist David Bohm, a protégé of Einstein, and Karl Pribram, a neurophysiologist at Stanford University and author of the classic neuropsychological textbook *Languages of the Brain*.

These two men formulated their ideas and theories over several decades of work. Pribram published his first article on the possible holographic nature of the brain in 1966 and continued to expand and refine his ideas during the next several years. Bohm studied the principle of interconnectedness and eventually became convinced that the universe actually employed holographic principles in its operation—that the universe itself is a kind of giant, flowing hologram. He published his first papers on his holographic view of the universe in the early 1970s.

Intriguingly, Bohm and Pribram arrived at their conclusions independently and while working from two very different directions. Bohm became convinced of the universe's holographic nature only after years of dissatisfaction with the standard theories' inability to explain all of the phenomena encountered in quantum physics. Pribram became convinced because of the failure of standard theories of the brain to explain various "neurophysiological puzzles."

As you read *Holographic Golf,* you will be learning some new terms, two of which are most important and relevant to our applications. They are *implicate* and *explicate* order. To explain these terms and develop their relevancy to our methods, we turn to Michael Talbot's *The Holographic Universe* and take a look at some of David Bohm's findings. In the 1960s Bohm was led to take a closer look at *order.* Classical science generally divides things into two categories: those that possess order in the arrangement of their parts and those whose parts are disordered, or random, in arrangement. Snowflakes, computers, and living things are all ordered. The pattern a handful of spilled coffee beans makes on the floor, the debris left by an explosion, and a series of numbers generated by a roulette wheel are all disordered. As Bohm delved more deeply into the matter, he realized there were also different degrees of order. Some things were much more ordered than other things, which implied that there was, perhaps, no end to the hierarchies of order that existed in the universe. From this it occurred to Bohm that maybe things that we perceive as disordered aren't disordered at all. Perhaps their order is of such an "indefinitely high degree" that they only appear to us as random (interestingly, mathematicians are unable to prove randomness, and although some sequences of numbers are categorized as random, these are only educated guesses). While immersed in these thoughts, Bohm saw a device on a BBC television program that helped him develop his ideas even further. The device was a specially designed jar containing a large rotating cylinder. The narrow space between the cylinder and the jar was filled with glycerine—a thick, clear liquid—and floating motionlessly in the glycerine was a drop of ink. What interested Bohm was that when the handle on the cylinder was turned, the drop of ink spread out through the syrupy glycerine and seemed to disappear. But as soon as the handle was turned back in the opposite direction, the faint tracing of ink slowly collapsed upon itself and once again formed a droplet.

Bohm writes, "This immediately struck me as very relevant to the question of order since when the ink drop was spread out, it still had a 'hidden' (i.e., non-manifest) order that was revealed when it was reconstituted. On the other hand, in our usual language, we would say that the ink was in a state of disorder when it was diffused through the glycerine. This led me to see that new notions of order must be involved here."

One of Bohm's most startling assertions is that the tangible reality of our everyday lives is really a kind of illusion, like a holographic image. Underlying it is a deeper order of existence, a vast and more primary level of reality that gives birth to all the objects and appearances of our physical world in much the same way that a piece of holographic film gives birth to a hologram. Bohm calls this deeper level of reality the *implicate*, which means "enfolded," order, and he refers to our own level of existence as the *explicate*, or unfolded, order.

The golf shots that you, in your average mode, produce are in explicate form. The really great shots that you only rarely produce and the smooth, good-feeling practice swings that you take are located in the implicate order of your capabilities. It took science a long time to figure out the laser and to figure out how to evoke the explicate order out of a piece of holographic film, and now it is time to discover how to evoke our best shots and our best swings out of the implicate order of the potential we all possess.

Introduction

THE GOLF SWING, through the years, has been dissected to the point of exhaustion. It has been extensively studied by experts from every field and by the unerring freeze-frame capabilities of the video camera.

All of this has been to no avail, as millions of confused duffers well know. They still search for the "secret"—the one magic move that will transform them into great players. The truth is that golf instruction is not only stagnant, but ineffective. There are many great communicators and motivators, but no real innovators. Most improvement has been a result of better equipment and more well-manicured golf courses.

Now, at last, innovation is here! Not innovation for the sake of variety, but innovation that works. Golf instruction will never be the same, and henceforth we will have to redefine what good play is. Throw away your stacks of instructional articles and enter this new, exciting dimension of development with an open mind, a blank slate.

As we begin to etch upon your empty piece of holographic film, and your true potential begins to emerge, you will be left with your own golf hologram, a reality that will translate into better performance with much less complication.

I strongly suggest that while you read this book you read two other books: Michael Murphy's *Golf in the Kingdom* and Michael Talbot's *The Holographic Universe*. Those two books together provided the catalyst for this book called *Holographic Golf*.

Shivas today?

The New Basics:

Interconnectedness and the Three Static Positions

A GOLF BALL lies on the ground, motionless. The target, also motionless, lies waiting. The golfer holds his club, steps to the ball, and swings the club.

Every golfer, from the world's very best to the novice, has known the artistry involved in a well-struck golf shot. The flowing swing, the chain reaction of smooth, sequential movements, the feeling of centrifugal force, and the sight of the ball hurtling toward the target, hanging against the sky, and gently dropping down. It's this scenario which hooks us to the game.

Performing such artistry is like knowing a moment of genius and briefly transcending our mortal abilities. It's as if somehow, for some reason, a deeply buried potential surfaces from the implicate order and is manifested. Sometimes it lingers, but more often it retreats to its hiding place until conditions are right for its return to *our* reality, the explicate order.

Holographic Golf is about discovering the implicate order and how to reach it. It is about extending our glimpse of genius and evoking our potential for artistry.

The world's great players who consistently strike the ball well have coaxed the abilities of their implicate order through many years of repetition and devotion and *never* give it a chance to retreat. They practice constantly, most of them daily. When these players stay away from the game for an extended period of time, their abilities fade and diminish and they become latent again in the implicate order.

By combining our knowledge of the *physical* mechanics of swinging a golf club with the emerging concept of the holographic universe, it is possible to harness our full potential. That is what this book is about.

Come with me to the practice tee with your mind a blank slate and let's discover the reality of your potential. The golf swing is just that, a swing. We swing the golf club—with that swing we propel the ball toward a target. It doesn't matter if that target is a fraction of an inch from the ball or hundreds of yards away—the swing must be on the correct plane so that we can control the direction of the ball and powerful enough to reach faraway targets. Each swing, however, begins from a static or motionless position.

The Three Static Positions

The first of the three static positions involves aim, alignment, and balance. It can be altered, molded, shaped, and changed from swing to swing. This position is called the *address position*. Present-day golf instruction (and all previous instruction) is fundamentally and universally ineffective because it fragments the motion portions of the swing, rearranges them, and asks the students to fit them back together. This method simply does not work. The *motion* parts of the golf swing cannot be worked on. The swing is a direct result of what exists in the three static positions. Remember the first static position, the *address*. The second is the *position at the top*, the point where the backswing in motion ends and the downswing in motion begins. The third static position is the *finish*.

The finish, as we shall discuss later, is also where the chain reaction begins because the golf swing is interconnectedness (where all things influence and are influenced by all others) at its best, proving that fragmentation is a futile myth.

To understand the interconnectedness of the golf swing and the *two-way* chain reaction, look at the finish, the third static position. Often I ask students with poor mechanics to concentrate on finishing properly and with good form.

By finishing with good form and ignoring the rest of the swing, an amazing thing occurs. All of the mechanics necessary to bring the player to a formful, balanced finish are performed automatically! The earlier in-motion portions of the golf swing cannot be fragmented or worked on separately because the swing happens too quickly. To illustrate:

A number of years ago several tour players were asked to hit drivers (the swing with the longest arc and longest elapsed time) and were told to abort their swing when they saw a strobe light flash. They could not see or anticipate the light's random flashes. Not one player was able to abort the swing after the club head had traveled more than two feet! The experiment concluded that the moving swing happens too fast for the mind to alter it once it's under way.

The study concluded that whenever you see a player abort a swing, either the player had made the decision to abort *before* the swing began or something physically stopped or interrupted the swing (grass, twig, rock). This also shows that the moving parts of the golf swing, the parts in motion, will continue in motion until they reach a static position. When the static positions are of poor quality, there is little chance for anything more than an occasional lucky shot due to simple eye-hand coordination. But with quality static positions, even nonathletes can produce consistently good golf shots.

STATIC POSITION NUMBER ONE: THE ADDRESS, OR SETUP
Let's move to the first static position, the address, or setup, and see how it can influence

the motion for the next phase of your swing (Figures 1 and 2).

When you learn the game's fundamentals, you learn to hold the club and stand to the ball with the club placed directly behind it. You are taught to aim properly. The instructor then attempts to show you how to start the motion part of the swing, called the "initial take-away." Right there, the process of fragmentation has begun, a process that will lead the golfer on a wild goose chase. Quite often in instruction two other fragmentations occur immediately thereafter: (1) "Keep the right elbow in close to the body," and (2) "Begin hinging your wrists when your hands reach waist-high."

Figures 1 and 2: The Address position from a side view (Figures 1, at left) and from the front (Figure 2).

The player will spend the rest of his or her golfing career trying to get the fragments right, fussing over separate portions of the motion, always trying to make the "right move." The golfer is encouraged by the few good shots he makes per round. What the player does not realize is that because golf involves eye-hand coordination, good shots can *sometimes* be struck due to random hit-or-miss compensation.

To hit good shots consistently requires good mechanics, and good mechanics start with perfecting the three static positions. Every player knows that top golfers, when addressing the ball, *look* like they know what they're doing. Like Shivas Irons, the mystical hero and sensational golf guru in *Golf in the Kingdom*, they seem to be "summoning up building energy" as the "concentration wells." Witness the awkward duffer, however, who addresses the ball with *poor form*, uncertainty, even fear. The difference is obvious. The good player has a grip that is unified, comfortable, and secure. The stance or *foundation*, as I call it, is balanced and relaxed, but reactive.

Aim and alignment are extremely important. When you pull the trigger on a rifle, the barrel must be aimed at the target if you expect the bullet to hit the target. In golf, the club face is the barrel, and the bullet (golf ball) will be propelled from that club face. You must aim the club face, not your body, at the target. The body lines (feet, knees, hips, and shoulders) should be very close, if not exactly parallel, to your target line (the line from your ball to the target). This first static position is critical. If you are aimed poorly, one of two undesirable results will ensue.

First, if you make a good swing, the ball will miss the target. Or, second, you will try to compensate for poor aim with a manipulative swing. Practice assuming a correct address position and take pictures of it. Compare them to the positions of good players, then compare them to the positions of very poor players. Note the visual differences, then adjust accordingly. When your picture agrees visually with the top players, when you feel balanced, comfortable, reactive, and show good form, take more pictures. While carefully studying the final pictures, practice assuming your correct address position in front of a mirror.

Take great care while following this process, for this address position—the first static position—is the beginning of the chain reaction that will follow.

I want to tell you that for every thousand students I teach, *maybe* five have an excellent address position! Once you are in that one-half percent, however, everything will become possible. My experience has taught me, almost without exception, that when a world-class player gets a bad result, it is due to poor aim or alignment, because he swings virtually the same way every time.

STATIC POSITION NUMBER TWO: AT THE TOP

Now we have reached the fork in the road where we break from the traditional line of instruction which continues to fragment the motion of the golf swing. *Holographic Golf* takes us to the next static position—the top of the swing (Figures 3 and 4).

Figures 3 and 4: At-the-Top position shown from the side (Figure 3, at left) and from the front (Figure 4).

This position *can* be fragmented, however, just like the address position, because it is not in motion—it is between motions just like the address.

The address position is the time between the motions of walking up to your ball and the motion of swinging at it. The position at the top is the time after your backward swing and before your forward swing. These static positions can be molded and shaped to *influence* the motion segments. The motion segments of the golf swing are *totally* dependent on the static positions; yet, golf instruction has forever tap-danced around this fact.

Enormous amounts of instructional material teaches students to "swing from the inside," "start the hips down first," "delay the hands." How can you delay the hands consciously when you can't even abort a swing that is only two feet underway?

Our fork in the road takes us to the second static position: the position at the top, also called the change of direction or the top of the backswing. You must be balanced, and your left arm should still be extended as it was at address. This is to ensure the width of your arc. You see, books can go on for pages about every minute detail of the position at the top, but if you're balanced and perform the most basic fundamentals, every detail is achieved. Good balance eliminates many errors automatically.

Examples:
•You can't be balanced if you "sway."
•You can't be balanced if your height changes.
•You can't be balanced with no weight shift.

For static position number two, repeat the routine that you went through for the address position, with pictures, mirrors, and adjustments. When your position looks good *and* feels balanced, take your final picture.

STATIC POSITION NUMBER THREE: THE FINISH

The third static position, the finish (Figures 5 and 6), has some intriguing characteristics, and it has long fascinated me with its many applications pertaining to the whole entity of the swing. The finish is a culmination of all that went before. It is a result of efficient motion. The intriguing part, though, is that it can also *cause* efficient motion.

Figures 5 and 6: The Finish as seen from the front (Figure 5, at left) and from the side (Figure 6).

As stated before, the finish can be the end of the chain reaction, or it can be the beginning.

How can this be?

Because of another holographic principle called "the interconnectedness of all things."

The interconnectedness of the golf swing is

precisely why fragmentation does not and cannot work. I have conducted experiments with students who had struggled with numerous instructors who tried every way possible to teach them to "extend through the ball." Perhaps you have even struggled with this elusive concept yourself. In contrast, within ten minutes of showing the student how to simply *finish* with good form, I have seen students automatically swing with perfect extension through the ball. To achieve a good finish, one has to have extension. Because the entire swing is a chain reaction, achieving the third static position, the finish, *influences* the part of the motion that involves extension!

Take special care in constructing your third static position, the finish. The physical elements of a good finish are:

1) Weight mostly on your left leg (for right-handers) with that weight balanced between the left leg and your right toe.
2) Body facing the target, or just left of it.
3) Hands high.

The first characteristic, the weight being mostly on the left leg, is a result of a complete transfer of weight on the downswing. Being up on the right toe shows that the right leg and hip have released and fired through the hitting area. Your body (belt buckle or belly button are good keys) facing the target indicates that you have had complete body rotation through the swing.

High hands at the finish indicate full extension and good speed through the hitting area. These points will be reiterated and expanded on in chapter four.

Just as you did with the other two static positions, create your own finish based on the good form of top players, making sure that the above three characteristics are present. Practice swinging the club into a balanced, extended, and rotationally complete finish position.

Again, when it looks good and feels balanced and controlled, take your photographs.

You now have photographs of yourself showing good form and displaying sound fundamentals at the three static positions. These are the only three parts of the golf swing you will *ever* have to be concerned with. Everything else, all of the *moving* intervals, are simply a result of where you were at the static positions and the motion will flow in the direction dictated by those three key positions.

There are those who may argue that the position at the top is not really static—that there is some movement at all times once the swing is underway. They are mistaken. There must be a point where change of direction occurs. And that point, however brief, is static. In an interview not long ago, Byron Nelson (acknowledged by most everyone as one of the best ball-strikers of all time) had some interesting things to say about the position at the top. Nelson said that very few players, even good players, really *set* the club at the top well enough. In other words, most players rush back to the ball before they really *stop* the backswing and get set.

The *essence* of good timing in the golf swing is *not to rush*, to swing to the top, get set and balanced, then gradually accelerate to the ball. You can only accelerate to the ball with control if you are in a balanced, static position at the top, set to resume the motion which will carry you to the finish.

When you look at your photographs, or the jacket of this book, or any top player at the three static positions, you can sense the motion that exists between them. You can pick up the flow.

Let's go back to Byron Nelson and his observations regarding the top of the backswing and his belief that most players don't get set well enough. Since golf was invented, a universal mystery has existed regarding practice swings. Anyone who plays the game has been frustrated because his practice swing with no ball is better than his swing at the ball.

I'd like to relate an experience I had almost twenty-five years ago. I was teaching at a club up north, in Wisconsin, and one Sunday afternoon I was giving a clinic to a group of players from an NFL football team, many of whom had never played golf before. We were on the practice tee and I was wearing a microphone, hitting nine-iron shots and describing what I was doing as I went along, while they watched. After I had hit twenty-five or thirty balls and covered most of the basics, I turned to one of the players closest to me and handed him the club. I asked him to take a couple of swings (no ball) based on what he had seen and heard. He stepped up and, simply by mimicking me, made a fairly decent swing. It was somewhat crude, but it was fairly smooth, *unhurried*, and complete. I told him his effort was pretty darn good, and as I put a ball on the ground, I said, "Let's see you *hit* one."

It was early in my career, and I had no idea that what I had said would negatively program his mind (I would now say, "Let's see you *swing* at one").

As soon as I asked him to hit one he raised the club back over his shoulders and took a wild, hatchet-type chop at the ball and buried the nine iron in the ground!

I subsequently used that story in my teaching practice to get my students to "swing the club and let the ball get in the way of the swing" rather than to "hit the object," but, as good as it sounds, it doesn't work. The mind always knows that the ball is there. Instructors have tried to find the answer to this "hit versus swing" problem for as long as there has been golf instruction—to no avail. Now, thanks to the Holographic Principle of Interconnectedness, there is an answer.

Ball Flinging

For the past several months I have been conducting experiments with students trying out different ideas which have emerged from my study of the Holographic Principle of Interconnectedness. My students are at all levels of proficiency and physical characteristics. Finally, from an idea gleaned from *Golf in the Kingdom* and reinforced by principles from *The Holographic Universe*, I have developed a solution to the practice-swing mystery. In addition to solving the practice-swing problem, this concept has additional benefits.

This idea has been effective to such a high degree that students in session have become excited and literally joyful, as if they happened upon some great revelation. IT REALLY WORKS! All you need is a little visualization, a little concentration, and a little practice. Here is how it works.

As you address the ball, you imagine that the golf ball is highly magnetized and adheres to the club face as you begin your swing. The ball stays with your club as you move to the second static position, the top of the backswing (Figure 1). Now, as you move toward the finish, nearing the impact area, you "fling the ball" off of your club toward the target (Figure 2).

Almost from the first time you try this, you feel a wonderful sense of timing and smoothness of unforced motion.

You see, the real reason our swing at the ball is different from our practice swing is because we are in a hurry to hit it. On a practice swing, there is no ball and we are in no particular hurry, so we swing to the top, get set, collect ourselves with balance, and move to the finish. We take the time to get set at the top because there is no reason to hurry. Byron Nelson was on the right track with his observation, but the only way to overcome the mind's habits is to distract the mind with a positive replacement thought. This "magnetized ball" idea, with its "flinging" or "slinging" characteristic, also tends to slow down the backswing, which always results in better timing.

Figures 7 and 8: Ball Flinging. Figure 7 (left) shows the top of the swing; Figure 8 shows impact.

There is another extremely valuable result gained from this concept. When the player flings the ball off of the club face at impact, an amazing thing occurs, and I have observed this phenomenon with high-speed video analysis. The idea of flinging the ball off of the club face results in a perfectly executed release of the hands, something every golfer has agonized over at one time or another. It is one of the questions most frequently asked by students. "Am I releasing correctly?" "Show me how I should release." How can you fragmentally show someone something that occurs in a split second at very high speed? You can't, but if the student moves from a correct static position number two to a correct static position number three and employs a concept such as ball flinging, then that elusive mechanical mystery of releasing correctly happens automatically. You see, as Shivas Irons says, you must be "one with the ball," interconnected and not fragmented away from it.

If the ball becomes fragmented from the symphony of our movements, then its presence as an outside force will disrupt the rhythm of our swings. Shivas Irons said to think of the ball and the "sweet spot" of the club face belonging together. He said to think of them "already joined." He said to imagine them fitting together as you lay the club head behind the ball. You can see the tie-in to the Holographic Principle of Interconnectedness. Shivas Irons, like Byron Nelson, was hot on the trail of one of golf's mysteries.

Now, let's take the new basics of Holographic Golf and put them to work. These new basics, the three static positions, are the blueprint for the construction of your new golf swing. Very soon your old mechanical, robotlike movements will be replaced with a free-flowing, fluid motion—a fluidity that is highlighted and guided (and caused) by the formful, balanced static positions.

Once I have my students in a comfortable, correct, and balanced address position, and once they can visually confirm it and *feel* it when it is visually correct, they will stay on-plane, maintain width of arc, and hinge the wrists correctly. It is that simple.

There is no need to think of a "one-piece take-away" or "cocking the wrists" or "taking it back low and straight." If you reach static position two correctly and started from a correct static position one, the only way in between is the right way!

In chapter five, on practice, I will provide some helpful drills to enable you to add motion to your correct static positions.

2

Static Position Number One:
The Setup and Its Preparation

THE ADDRESS POSITION in golf is the "first brick," the "programming of the computer," the foundation. It is the piece of holographic film waiting for instruction, for the imprints and guidelines from which creativity will emerge.

It is the first step, and it must be a sound one. To illustrate the importance of this starting position, I want you to think back and recall your "best rounds," your "best shots ever" and remember how comfortable you were as you addressed the ball and began your swing. It is very characteristic of players on all levels that when they feel confident and comfortable over the ball, they usually make good swings.

But when you recall your slumps, your times of confusion, and your bad shots, you will realize that you were very uncomfortable and uncertain over the ball and that your swing felt bad and far from smooth and fluid.

I can honestly say that whenever I've felt good over the ball—and I will expand on the term "good" later in the chapter—I have almost without exception hit good shots.

There are volumes and volumes of instructional pieces and indeed almost entire books on how to set up or address the ball. Most of these writings instruct the player to place the feet shoulder-width for the driver. I have actually seen in a published golf book a chart illustrating where to place the ball in the stance with each club needing a specific spot in the stance.

These, of course, are suggestions, but they are potentially damaging. It's like buying suits off the rack—they may or may not fit very well.

The very first thing that each beginning golfer (or any golfer wishing to improve) must know is that the game of golf is extremely individualized, to the point where the *individual* dictates the best method. Certainly effective mechanics always have parameters, but with golf these parameters are wide and flexible. As Shivas Irons said, "No two swings are ever alike," and I believe that this is true even for the world's greatest players. No two shots in golf are ever alike. Conditions are always changing.

This endless variety is part of golf's intrigue—what makes the game so interesting. On every shot we hit, even from almost identical positions on the course, there are constant subtle changes to be considered: wind, humidity, time of day, soil conditions, grass conditions, contour, pin position, slope. These are just some of the factors which affect golf shots (and swings).

Then, of course, there are the human factors, which change with each passing second.

The point, as you can begin to see, is that golf is far from being an exact science, written in stone. Methods cannot be blindly and universally applied. We don't just walk up and hit wonderful golf shots consistently, we must create them and *plan* them.

We can only approach real consistency through planning and factoring in as many variables as are available to us. The ball lies motionless, and so does the target. For the ball to be effectively sent to the target, there are obstacles to avoid and "helping currents" to take advantage of. The beginning position is the one big chance to gather this data and formulate a plan because once the motion of the swing is underway, it is a fluid result of a static position and cannot be substantially altered until the next attempt. If you consistently start poorly, you will consistently swing poorly.

Feeling Good at the Address

From conversations with many tour players, and from my own experience, it seems that feeling good over the ball involves several factors. First, the golf club feels good in your hands. The club should feel light and well balanced, and you should be able to feel "one with the club." Obviously, taking great care when outfitting yourself with a set of golf clubs is extremely important. It is recommended that you try many different sets before you settle on the best-feeling clubs. The next factor is the relationship between your body and the ground. The importance of this relationship cannot be overstated because your balance is influenced by this important connection.

You have to experiment with the width of your stance, ball position, and even posture, just as you experimented before you bought your clubs, until you feel balanced, comfortable, and reactive, yet sturdy (see Figures 1 and 2). All the manuals say that your stance should be shoulder-width and your posture should be bent slightly from the waist, knees slightly flexed and back straight. But remember, that manual cannot see *you*, and variations usually are necessary to accommodate differences in anatomy and flexibility.

There are two more factors which influence how we feel over the ball, and they have nothing to do with the "static mechanics" of grip and stance. But first, getting back to the way the club feels in our hands, we must discuss the way we hold the club—the grip.

The grip tormented me for many years. I felt that there were times, especially after a short layoff, or while I was in a slump, that my hands were somehow out of position on the club. I would constantly experiment and adjust, but the experimenting never worked. I looked at my fellow touring pros and noted how many different-looking grips there were among the world's best players.

It gradually dawned on me, after many years, that these players all had different grips that were *similar*, but that exact positioning of the hands on the club is simply not the answer to having the club consistently feel good. This consists of a combination of things: one, clubs that fit, that generally feel good; two, a grip that is *somewhere near* the neutral position, that is, palms facing and perpendicular to the target line. But, most of all, the secret to having the club consistently feel good in your hands is to actually have a club in your hands a good portion of every day.

At this point, I want to recommend two things to all golfers at all levels. First, purchase one of those hand and wrist strengtheners, and use it a little each day. Second, get a golf club that you will never use and cut the shaft several inches below the grip. Tape the end to avoid scratches and cuts. Carry this with you—in the car, into the TV room, and when you get a few seconds or minutes, grip the club over and over. Just feel the grip whenever you think of it. I guarantee you, you will keep your feel from day to day and the club will feel much more comfortable in your hands on a regular basis. If this can work for the pros, you can make it work for you!

Now other factors come into play with regard to how we feel over the ball, factors which we seemingly cannot control. But keeping in mind the reality of a holographic figure and how an entire level of reality (such as a dream) can be conjured up by the mind and senses, we *can* control factors which seem to control and direct us.

Let's say that your stance feels good—solid, reactive, balanced—and the club feels great in your hands. You're standing over a four-iron shot to a well-trapped, but accessible green. Confidence is riding high, and the way you feel over the ball complements that confidence.

As you prepare to begin the swing and look toward the target, the wind suddenly picks up and causes you to back away. You then realize that a weather front is moving through and the temperature is dropping rapidly as the winds increase. You reassess your club selection and reach for the three iron, wondering if even that is enough club as the wind blows harder and quarters from left to right and against you. While considering your club selection and realigning your shot, you notice something that you hadn't noticed before—your lie is slightly sidehill with the ball a little below your feet.

As you can see, what only moments before

was an easy-looking shot that you were approaching with confidence has suddenly become a difficult one. Your setup is fraught with negatives, and, even worse, you have less feel for the club in your fingers, which are cold and numb. This is but one example of how outside forces, some physical and real and some intangible or imagined, can suddenly and drastically change your outlook and confidence level, and, worse yet, how the club feels in your hands or how your connection to the ground feels. It is amazing how fragile the golf swing is, especially when the mind is looking for and dwelling on negative influences.

I am convinced that the really great players are able through concentration and positive imagery to overcome not only potentially negative factors, but to turn them into positives. In one of Jack Nicklaus's books, he said that as he prepares to hit a shot, he sees an image in his mind of himself sitting at home in his recliner watching himself on his television preparing to hit the shot, hitting it, and seeing the desired result. He then proceeds to hit the shot. That use of imagery is powerful, and I believe it helped make Nicklaus the player he is.

Imagery of that sort sounds simple, but to develop it fully and to the point where it is consistently effective takes as much practice as Nicklaus ever did on his grip, stance, or swing.

Think back over the times when your golf

game was at its best—when every hole seemed to just flow to the next, with every drive down the fairway and iron shots that were solid. Even putts required almost no thought. You were in a groove.

Now think to the times of your worst slumps, when you couldn't hit any shot, even short pitches. Your swing felt as if it were in pieces with a hundred movements, all out of sync. Examine your thoughts in each instance and compare the tremendous differences. When you're playing and swinging your best, you are, as Shivas Irons says, "letting the nothingness into your swing." But when you're slumping and no part of your game feels good, then that smooth "nothingness," that effortless rhythm, is replaced with every golfing demon that the mind can conjure up.

Concentration, Imagery, and the Trance of Routine

Now for dealing with those demons which, take note, come forth *before* we ever swing. Static position number one, as you can see, involves far more than posturing and positioning. Concentration, of course, is the weapon against these negative factors. Concentration comes from a set plan, a *routine* that never varies. This routine not only involves physical movements as we prepare to address the ball, but also things like imagery—the positive imagery of Jack Nicklaus.

Shivas Irons says that negative thoughts should be met head-on, embraced, explored, and then blended into our positive imagery so that we emerge over the ball relaxed, at peace, confident. If you watch very closely as a professional prepares to address the ball, you will see that the routine never varies.

It is as if once the club selection is completed and it is his turn to play, a button is pressed and the "trance of routine and concentration" begins. This "trance" remains apparent until the ball comes to rest. The whole golfing world is familiar with players like Ben Hogan and Ray Floyd and the look in their eyes when they were in contention. Their concentration was so intense that they seemed unaware of any extraneous sounds.

When you see a player complain about a photographer clicking a camera, check his score and you'll see how harmful poor concentration can be. Just imagine the effect on the average player whose fundamentals are not as sound to begin with.

The Holographic Principle of Interconnectedness is never more evident than when you prepare to address the ball, because once it is your turn to hit, until the shot comes to rest, there should be one continuous stream of concentration. As we go on to discuss the two other static positions, the guiding checkpoints of our technique, you will see how everything can blend together, producing that effortless, yet powerful and flowing feeling that we experience when we strike our best shots.

It is important to stress the importance of watching the shot until it comes to rest whenever possible. By doing this we experience valuable feedback. We see how the ball flies under the present conditions, we relate the feel of the swing to the flight of the ball, we see how the ball bounces and how that relates to the way it flew and to the swing, and how the terrain affected the bouncing of the ball. A visual imprint of all these effects is etched into our memories.

If some time in the future we are faced with a *similar* shot under *similar* conditions, whether consciously aware of it or not, we draw from that experience and incorporate its "feel" into the thought process and swing.

This is why it is so very important for any aspiring player to practice an endless variety of shots under all sorts of conditions. Every shot, every swing, regardless of the outcome, in some way influences future attempts. It is important to focus on positive aspects of a shot or swing, and this leads us to how the role of positive imagery and *blending* (which will be discussed later) can help overcome those golfing demons, those negative thoughts that always bring disastrous results.

Using positive imagery is one of those things that sounds and seems simple, but is quite difficult to execute. Clearly, one of the keys to making it work is to incorporate it into a consistent routine of addressing the ball.

An important aspect of this routine is to focus on details such as club selection, lie, terrain, and atmospheric conditions.

This last detail, obviously, can change in seconds and require a new club selection. But for almost all shots, you should already have considered these factors before your routine begins.

Dancing Through the Shot

Other vital components of the routine and concentration are cadence, balance, and feeling the ground and golf club. Watch a great player go through his preshot routine from start to finish and you'll see a dance. This is so evident that if you watch a great player hit enough shots, you'll pick up the cadence and literally "dance through the shot" with the player. It is important to develop a cadence, a rhythm of your own, one with which you are comfortable. Perhaps you can develop the rhythm of *your* routine by emulating the rhythm of a fine player. Have you ever noticed that after watching golf on television, your swing feels really good? It's because you've picked up the cadence of the great players. It goes away because you don't focus on it during your *own* performance. You can develop this simply by working on it consciously and letting go of your negative focusing on fears.

Watch a good player dance through the shot and you'll see the feet shifting and moving rhythmically the same way every time. Watch the hands feel the club. The player is picking up signals from the ground, signals that join the player's cadence as they are transmitted through the player to the feel of the club head, which is the only thing that contacts the ball. The surgeon's scalpel may make the incision, but think of the knowledge, experience, and training that is collectively transmitted to that knife. An absolutely vital aspect of your routine is that it be exactly the same every time. Whether the routine you adopt contains the elements discussed is totally up to you.

But it must be repetitive to the point of being indistinguishable from shot to shot, regardless of the club or shot you're playing. You will be amazed at how much more consistent your swing will be if your preshot routine is consistent. Watch a great player with a great attitude, like Tom Kite, stride up the eighteenth fairway and go through his preshot routine. You cannot tell if he is eight under par or eight over par. His method never varies. Watch an eighteen handicapper and you'll usually see the precision and purposefulness of the first tee shot of the round degenerate into a wild, careless swipe at the ball as the player reaches the last part of the round. His swing didn't leave him—his routine and his concentration wavered and then fell out of sight.

Blending

Now, let's discuss "blending." I have (and so have many other professionals) used blending for many years, but I'd like to quote a passage from *Golf in the Kingdom* that embodies the totality of the concept and puts into words what other players and I have utilized and experienced:

Aikido is a Japanese art of self-defense. Robert Nadeau is a teacher of this subtle art who lives and works near San Francisco, and in recent months he has helped me bring the principles of it into my golf game. Although he has never played the game himself, he has an amazing grasp of its problems and opportunities. "Blending," for example, is a way to join yourself with your opponent's strength in order to divert his attack; when used correctly it turns a fight to a dance. He has shown me how to "blend" my strength with club, ball, and terrain on the course, in the same way I join with attackers during an Aikido class. It works surprisingly well. Perhaps the most impressive thing about it has been the way in which it has helped me adapt my swing to every situation. My repertoire of shots has grown because I have learned to go with the dynamics of air, wind, and slope, using the energies of the situation to help rather than hinder me. Shivas had said to find my "original swing" in every situation, claiming that he never swung the same way twice. It was hard for me to see the deviation in his flawless strokes, but he claimed they were there. The "blending" principle has brought that subtle adaptation of method to situation into play for me. An old letter Shivas had never mailed to some student or friend was among the papers I photographed in his apartment. It is a small essay on blending. Shivas says:

"Can you see the brook that golfers fear and not fearing, but feeling, can you put that flowing water into your swing." What a beautiful way to say it. I think of his swing as I read these words and realize what grace and what strength there is in such "blending."

Now, let's go back to our four-iron shot, where the wind has come up and is quartering left to right and the temperature is falling as fast as your confidence. Here is the perfect opportunity for "blending" and making potentially damaging negative factors work in your favor.

The game of golf, if you expect to play it well, demands this ability. The left-to-right wind, a little against you, combined with the falling temperature, will not allow the ball to travel as far. Instead of wondering how to force the four iron, or even if a three is enough club, seize the opportunity to use the four wood with a smooth, unforced swing, and aim the shot a little left. Even the cold temperature affords you the opportunity to rub your hands together, flex your fingers, and take a grip that is more secure than usual. You now are relaxed and confident in your club selection, you have the wind assisting you by pushing the ball *toward* the target, and your grip is secure and firm. What a different thought pattern this is from the usual "I have to force this club," "I have to fight this left-to-right wind," and "I can't feel the club—my fingers are getting numb." I like your chances a lot better with the first thought pattern.

Shivas's little essay on blending warrants more discussion and gives me the chance to offer a valuable tip utilizing blending. Having played in countless pro-ams, I have witnessed for many years how fear and negative focusing can destroy a player's concentration, confidence, and, ultimately, his swing. Let me relate a scene that I have witnessed many times:

Take a middle- to high-handicap player, who, when standing on the tee of a wide-open par four with no trouble in front of him or to either side, almost always hits a nice, solid drive. Put that same player on the same tee, but put a large lake directly in front of him requiring a carry of two hundred yards. Half the time, that same player will drive the ball into the lake. Depending on the degree to which the player "seizes up," as one of my students puts it, he will, out of fear brought on by negative focusing, either top or half-top the shot, or hit the ball off center of the club face and fall short of the fairway into the lake. I'd like to offer all of you who have suffered this indignation a cure—a cure made possible by blending.

The next time you find yourself in that situation, *before* your preshot routine, look directly at the water. See the waves or ripples. Failing that, see the stillness of the pond. See yourself floating on a raft in the lake and feel the tension leave your thoughts. Now press your button or hit your switch and go *immediately* into the trance of your preshot routine. You have blended the danger of the water into positive-thought focusing and prevented your muscles from tightening. It works. You can turn any golfing hazard into a plus if you just use your imagination. Just committing to using blending will help you right away. The game of golf is so mental!

A lot of our discussion of static position number one has involved the preshot routine and planning. The steps leading to the address position are all part of the programming necessary for effective swings. Without consistent planning, there will be no consistent performance. Sit down at a computer with no knowledge, no technique, and you may as well use a random generator. That's what golfers look like to me when they have no plan, no preshot routine, no consistency at the first static position.

And every shot they hit is different, as they slash their way around the course in hit-or-miss fashion with the accent on "miss." With careful preshot planning utilizing positive imagery, positive thought replacement by way of blending, and a rhythmic, dynamic preshot routine, you will confidently dance to the ball in a positive, relaxed state of concentration. You are at static position number one, and if you are relaxed, confident, and balanced, your fundamentals will now take over and guide you through your swing. We will now journey to static position number two, and upon arriving there we will look back and trace our steps to see how our arrival was guided and influenced by our beginning position. Remember one thing: the most important time in the golf swing is before it ever begins to move, but in Holographic Golf the movement really begins with the preshot routine and planning. In the golf swing, everything is a result of what went before—it is a chain reaction, it is interconnected, and you can blend anything into it for positive effect.

3

Static Position Number Two:
At the Top

THROUGH THE YEARS, there has been much discussion about the "top of the backswing," the "position at the top," and whether or not there really is a break in the motion.

The answer is that there is a break, a point before the change of direction, for the club cannot be moving in two directions at the same time. When you first learn the fundamentals of golf, you're taught the grip, the setup of the body, aim and alignment, and then the initial take-away and backswing. If all goes well, you reach a desirable position at the top.

Right here is where traditional golf instruction goes so wrong.

Too much attention and detail involving the *parts* of the take-away and backswing take the focus away from the static position at the top, which, not being a moving part, *can* be isolated and worked on. How can the initial take-away be isolated and worked on separately when it is but one aspect of a series of movements that are never at rest? Again, let's consider that if you practice and learn a good sound setup (static position one) and do the same with the position at the top (static position two), the *only* way to arrive at position two is to go from position one to position two with a mechanically correct initial take-away.

Now we are going to take a long look at this second static position and find out how it influences the forward swing, or downswing, which is the moving part of the *swing* (not hit) that finds the golf ball in its path.

In chapter one, we discussed how to assume static position one by watching top players. By doing so, you automatically incorporate certain fundamentally correct aspects of a sound address, such as left arm extended (for right-handed players) and knees flexed slightly.

Again, remember, these are *general* aspects and can slightly change from individual to individual, with regard to differences in anatomy, flexibility, and so on. The same holds true at the top of the swing (see Figures 3 and 4). For instance, some players' left arms are much straighter than others, and some players take the club back farther than others. These are individual differences resulting from individual differences in such capabilities as suppleness and flexibility. Note, however, that even a professional whose left arm is noticeably bent at the top has kept the arm as extended as possible. He or she may simply not be as flexible or supple as one whose arm appears perfectly straight. Generally speaking, with regard to what is fundamentally correct for the position at the top, please note the following:

1) Head *almost* in same position as at address.
2) Weight shifted to inside of right upper leg from an even distribution at address.
3) Left arm (for righties) extended but not rigidly stiff.
4) From address, shoulders have turned ninety degrees.
5) From address, hips have turned forty-five degrees.
6) Left shoulder under chin.
7) Left knee closer to right knee than at address.
8) Right elbow pointing to the ground.
9) Height unchanged from address.
10) Ninety-degree angle between left arm and club shaft.

We will now explore, in detail, these ten characteristics of a fundamentally sound static position number two and how they relate to the earlier and following movements in the swing.

The Head

Almost without exception, when golfers first take up the game, someone tells them, "Keep your head still." This is probably the most popular and often repeated golf cliché. But this advice can be very destructive to the beginner if it is not thoroughly explained. While it's true that the head should remain relatively still, overdoing it can restrict the body turn and subsequent weight shift and cause a loss of power in your shots.

In a good golf swing, there is some shifting of the weight, and when the weight shifts, there is bound to be *some* head movement. It's okay for the head to move *laterally*, but keep it minimal. The head has moved too far laterally only when the weight shifts to the outside edges of the feet.

I have always believed that it is far more detrimental to the golf swing for the head to move *vertically* during the swing. Any vertical movement results in changes in height, which then require compensatory movements. For instance, when there is upward vertical movement, getting back to the ball requires a *downward* dip, and, conversely, a downward vertical movement during the backswing will necessitate a straightening of the body in order to duplicate the position at address. Obviously, those kinds of adjustments are tricky to make, to say the least. One common thread that runs through the swings of good players is that there is little need for compensation. Their swings are efficient, simple, with little wasted motion. To start with a sound address, reach static position two soundly, and finish with balance, there must be little wasted motion and minimal compensation. At static position number one, you are striving for good balance as well as correct positioning. Good balance means equal distribution.

The Weight Shift

As you swing the club back to static position number two and the body turns (hips forty-five degrees, shoulders ninety degrees), some of the 50 percent of your weight that is on your left leg is transferred to your right leg. It is important that this weight transfer does not carry to the outside edge of your right foot. If it does, you will lose your brace, lose your balance, and require too much lateral compensation to get back to a balanced position. The forward swing will then be a desperate quest for balance instead of a smooth application of centrifugal force. You must shift enough weight to the right leg to "load up" the right side at the top of the swing, but not so much that the shift causes you to lose your right leg brace. Without a strong, balanced brace, there can be no powerful, efficient, and balanced thrust (known as "firing the right side") during the swing to the ball.

The Left Arm

Another of the time-worn clichés in golf is the oft-repeated "Keep your left arm straight." This is another of those many golf principles that is correct, sound advice, but only if explained in full. Like keeping the head still, a straight left arm can cause more harm than good if carried to extremes. The left arm should be extended as much as possible *without* locking at the elbow or to the point that it is tight and "clenched," or stiff. Keeping the arm extended yet reactive and supple helps give the arc its width, which is vital to building club-head speed. Without width of arc, the club contacts the ball with more of a *glancing* action and also potentially reduces the available time for the club head to gain speed. The game of golf has evolved to a power game due to equipment improvement and lengthening of golf courses. Years ago, as evidenced by the photographs of the top players, the left arm was noticeably bent at the top of the swing. That was because power was secondary and no great width of arc was necessary. You will find that with all good players today, the left arm begins in an extended position and remains that way well through impact. But remember, tight muscles are fatal to a fluid golf swing. When you see certain players with their left arms very straight, keep in mind that *how* straight your arm is at the top of your swing is simply a measure of your suppleness, or flexibility.

The arm is much straighter when you're seventeen than when you're fifty. Calvin Peete, who enjoyed a great run on the PGA Tour in the 1980s, displayed a position at the top with his left arm bent ninety degrees. That position, however, was due to an injury in his younger days which left his arm frozen at that angle. That was, for him, full extension of his arm. Some even attributed his prowess for accurate driving to the consistent status of his left arm.

The Shoulder Turn

At address, the shoulders are in a natural position. That is, they are not tilted or twisted one way or the other. Because the right hand is a few inches lower on the club than the left, the right shoulder will naturally be a little lower than the left. In order to wind up the spring (body) and store power which can be released when you unwind the spring, the torso, just like a spring, must twist back against resistance. We have already discussed how the right leg acts as a brace and provides that resistance. The torso winds up like a spring by employing certain actions of the hips, feet, legs, and shoulders.

We will discuss first how the shoulders do their part. Much has been written about the "shoulder turn," or "shoulder tilt." Taking either term literally will cause nothing but problems. If you just *turn* your shoulders, the club will describe an arc that is too flat or shallow and a pure tilt will result in a steep plane with no weight shift.

In reality, good players move their shoulders with a *combination* turn/tilt and move in this manner until the shoulders have moved ninety degrees from their position at address.

You can study any photograph of a good player and see that this movement is generally characterized by the back facing the target at the top of the swing. This is a necessary part of static position number two. If your back is facing the target at the top of the swing, your left shoulder is under your chin, your weight has shifted to the *inside* of your right *upper leg*, and you're balanced, then you have made an efficient backswing.

The Hips, Feet, and Legs

As the body and club start back from the ball, everything moves together. In good swings, the weight shift begins the moment that the motion begins. The left knee starts back and moves toward the right, and the hips start rotating until they've moved forty-five degrees from their starting position.

Because the shoulders have moved ninety degrees and the hips forty-five degrees, you can see how the coiling of your body—the spring—has occurred. This coil harbors energy, which is one of the main sources of power in the golf swing.

Keep in mind above everything else that the golf swing, from address to impact, is performed on the insides of the feet. At address, your knees should be pointed slightly in toward one another. This keeps you centered and aids balance. During the move to the top of the swing, shift to the inside of the right upper leg. If the inside sole of your right shoe leaves the ground as you move to the top, then you are losing your brace, losing your resistance, losing your coil, and your chance for accuracy and power will be lost.

Another checkpoint for an effective position at the top is the right elbow. It should be pointing at the ground with the right forearm in a vertical position. If you have made an efficient coil, and a balanced weight shift, you will notice *no* change in your height at the top of the swing from your address position. This is extremely important because it eliminates the need for compensation, which always results in wasted, unproductive motion.

I've saved for last the ninety-degree angle that you must create between the left arm and club-shaft at the top of the swing. Without this angle, there will not be enough power even to approach a quality golf shot. This angle is one of the most important components of the golf swing and a vital element of static position number two. A full (ninety-degree) shoulder turn/tilt and a proper hinging of the wrists are the keys to achieving this angle, which helps keep the club on an efficient path, or plane, and acts as a major source of power. We will see in the next chapter how this angle influences the quality of the swing from static position number two to static position number three, the finish.

Balance

At this point, I want to remind you that all of these details and swing parts are simply *characteristics* of efficient, correct golf swings. I do not want you to dwell on these details, but do try to make sure they are a part of your static position number two. As you develop your static positions, you will see that the only way to arrive efficiently at position two is to begin from a correct position one. Remember, the three sound, fundamentally correct static positions are the springboard and guideposts for powerful, controlled motion. Now, let's address the single most important characteristic of a sound static position number two, balance. It is a fact that many errors can be made in a golf swing, but if you stay fairly well balanced, you have a better chance of producing a good shot. On the other hand, you can do everything right and still hit a miserably poor shot if your balance is not good.

What I learned from Tommy Bolt, former U.S. Open champion, is that balance cannot be compromised. When you're playing football, tennis, basketball, soccer, you name it, and you lose your balance, you can regain it with the next step. In golf, there is no next step. When you lose your balance in a golf swing, that swing is ruined. If you do it enough times, there's a good chance your score will reflect lots of bogeys, double bogeys, and worse.

There is no such thing as a good golfer with poor balance, but there are poor athletes with good balance who are good golfers. When you practice achieving static position number two, keep this in mind: *you must have balance along with correct positioning*. When you are building your second static position and practicing it, make sure that you hold the position for more than a few seconds at a time and pay close attention to balance as you hold it. I cannot overstate how important this is, for without very good balance at the second static position, it is impossible to accelerate into the ball with the kind of power that is necessary for good shots. As we shall see in chapter four, power is generated by the use of centrifugal force and nothing can break down centrifugal force as fast as the loss of its constant, balanced center. So now we are at static position number two. We are in position and have coiled against resistance. We have a ninety-degree angle (or slightly more, but not at all less) between the left arm and the club shaft and the knees are closer together than they were at address. We are poised, balanced, and completely set. We have drawn a bead on the ball and are about to journey to static position three, a journey during which the ball will make contact with the accelerating club and be sent to the target.

4

Static Position Number Three:
The Finish and How We Arrive There

THE FINISH, SOME SAY, is a result of the swing,
an afterthought. The ball is gone, so what difference does the finish make? It's true that the finish
is a resultant position, indicative of the swing
that produced it. The finish, however, can also be
a cause of correct prior motion. Try this practice
method: set up at address, static position one,
with no ball. You're going to take a practice
swing. But instead of swinging back to position
two, swing to the finish from the address position. If your finish position is sound, balanced,
and formful, then the mechanics necessary to
give you that result *had to occur!* If you practice
putting yourself into a correct finish position
enough times, your prior motions will improve
dramatically. First, we will examine in detail, as
we did with static position two, what constitutes
an effective, formful, balanced finish position,
and we will then explore the motional area

between positions two and three, the area where contact with the ball is made. Study photographs of the good players—the pros and fine amateurs—and you'll quickly notice the similarities in their finishes. Most of the weight has moved to the left leg, with any right-side weight balanced on and anchored by the right toe-tip of the golf shoe. The belt buckle (or belly button) is facing the target and the hands are rather high (some players finish high, and then drop down some into a *relaxed* finish position).

Landing at Static Position Number Three

Let's take these characteristics one at a time and examine their meaning. First, your weight has finished mostly on your left leg (see Figure 3). Remember static position two, where your weight has shifted from address (equally distributed) to the inside of the right leg (see Figure 4). The right side has been "loaded." That loading was achieved by coiling, specifically coiling the lower body, which moved some weight to the right leg. As the body, after its stopover at position two, begins to unwind the other way, the weight that was loaded is fired back to the left as the body unwinds and the hips rotate toward the target (see Figure 5). Part of this unwinding is the driving (like a piston) of the right leg and hip to the target. This shifting of weight, which helps pull the hands and club into and through the impact zone, is one major producer of centrifugal force and club-head speed. Imagine a boxer throwing a punch while moving backward. There won't be much power in that punch. Be it tennis, boxing, baseball, golf, or any sport where an object is going to be struck, the blow must move *into* the object to be struck. This blow can only reach maximum power levels when every source of power is used to deliver it.

I have seen many fine golf swings that had every ingredient necessary for consistency and accuracy, but lacked sufficient power for high-level play. When it comes to golf, *everyone* has the potential to produce good club-head speed, but most people don't know how. Using the body weight effectively is one major method of generating club-head speed. Good players finish with their belt buckles (or belly buttons) facing either the target or just left of it (see Figure 6). Assuming a complete coiling at static position two, this finish position indicates that there has been a full rotation of the hips and torso. At this point, let's take a look at centrifugal force and how it applies to the golf swing.

We've all seen a row of ice skaters with arms linked going around the ice in a big circle. The inside skater is barely moving, but she acts as the hub of this big wheel. If she stays steady and the line stays intact, the outside skater is circling the arena at great speed. Well, as you address the ball in golf, the inside skater is your center, your center of balance. The outside skater is the club head. The swing must emanate from your center, which must remain steady, balanced, in control. If it does, and the linking mechanisms in the swing remain intact (in control), then the club head, as a result of centrifugal force, will zip through the air with great speed. Your hips are part of the center of the swing, and they must rotate efficiently and *fully*. Remember, on the backswing your hips face away from the target, in a balanced stance, and then rotate to the finish position. Your hips are the first link in the chain that is working to produce centrifugal force and maximum club-head speed.

Another characteristic of a good golf swing, and part of a formful static position three, is high hands at the finish. This is a result of three things. First, it indicates that there was good arm extension at and after impact; second, that there was strong acceleration of the club head in the hitting area. Remember, good full arm extension insures the width of arc and maximizes the time in which the club has the opportunity to accelerate. This is the reason that most flat, shallow, and short swings are weaker and do not produce a great deal of power. The third cause of a desirable "high hands finish" is good club-head speed through the hitting area. This momentum through the ball, combined with complete rotation and a wide arc, carries the hands to a high finish position. When you see a player finish with *low* hands, it indicates either very low club-head speed, no extension with the club being pulled across the body, or a swing plane that is too flat or shallow.

Study the finish position of good players, and begin to incorporate the characteristics that you see into your own technique. Confirm your work with pictures. As you begin to finish with good form and balance, you'll see the motion segment between your finish and your position at the top begin to improve.

When Static Positions Two and Three Are of Good Quality, Here's What Happens in Between

Remember static position number two and how you've coiled against resistance while maintaining balance and control. You've also achieved the widest possible arc with the club head due to full extension while retaining balance. You are now at static position two, set at the top, poised and ready to move to static position three, the finish. This move will be a controlled, measured one, but within that control great acceleration of the club head will occur. *Centrifugal force and stored energy* make it possible to generate sufficient club-head speed to propel the ball long distances.

So here we are, poised and set at the top.

What happens next? Let's go back a little and recall that the swing emanates from the center, from your physical center. Just as your back-swing coil began from your center and slowly spread *outward,* your *uncoiling* must begin from this same center. The hips are the largest part of this center, and they are the first part of your body to unwind. The real heart of an effective golf swing is this winding and unwinding, which extends from a *center* to the club head.

You have already learned how to include the ball in your swing, and this should be a part of the entire motion. If the ball is not included, it then becomes an object to *hit at* and this thought disrupts the fluid and gradual buildup of club-head speed.

Balancing Your Center from Two to Three

Just as important as including the ball in your swing from your center is keeping this center *very steady.* Balance promotes consistent eye-hand coordination and affords a better chance of hitting the sweet spot of the club face. Re-member, there is a very important distinction to be made here between the words *steady* and *still.* You do not ever want to strive to keep your center (or head) *still.* Doing so will only result in a restricted movement with an abbrevi-ated or false turn and an inadequate weight shift, or, even worse, a reverse weight shift.

If you keep your balance as you coil and uncoil and swing from the *insides* of the feet, however, your center will remain steady, with only minimal movement—movement that is a natural by-product of a "coil and shift" motion. As your hips begin the unwinding process, your legs go with them and your upper torso feels the pull of the lower body and begins to unwind. Next come the arms, hands, and club shaft. All of this pulling motion results in a chain reaction, with the club-head as the final link. Think of a bullwhip. There is not much violent or visible force applied as your hand cracks the whip, but the tip is the last link in the chain reaction effect and flies at tremendous speed as it cracks. When you swing a golf club effectively, the same thing occurs. You don't see any violent force or action as the calm center begins the chain reaction, but when you do it properly, the club head, just like the tip of the bullwhip, attains very high speeds.

Let's go back to static position two and recall the extended left arm and the ninety-degree angle that it forms with the club shaft. Your wrists have hinged fully, thereby making this angle possible. While your hips, torso, and shoulders all pull as the spring unwinds and the weight shifts, this angle is preserved, and even momentarily *increased*, as the uncoiling unfolds.

It is the initial retention of this angle that unlocks the ultimate source of power. This angle, when it is retained well into the down-swing, is a storehouse of energy and power. When it is released as the swing nears the ball, the energy stored within it is unleashed and the club head accelerates. Preserving this angle well into the downswing can make very long drivers out of small, physically weak people, and failing to preserve it can make very short drivers out of strong, gifted professional athletes.

Reassuming the Address Position with Your Hips

As your hips make their initial move to begin the unwinding process, note that they reassume the position they were in at address or position one. They are "square" or parallel to the target line. This reassuming of the address position is critical to keeping the arc wide and preserving good, full extension. Many poor players skip this move and go directly from the top into a "spin move" with the hips. This pulls the arms across the body, destroys the width of the arc, reduces extension, and results in a low, poor finish. If static position two is correct and static position three is correct, then all of the correct movements, such as "preserving the angle" and "reassuming the address position" occur automatically. They have to. It's the same thing with "fire the right side." If you finish with your weight on your left leg and your belly button facing the target, then you *had* to have fired the right side, but, if you consciously try to work on things like "preserving the angle" or "firing the right side," then that's about all you'll accomplish. What about the other ten characteristics that have to occur? Do you think there is enough time during the down-swing to think of and work on all of these moves? Of course not, but by now you should begin to see the real picture and start to let go of your preoccupation with "swing fragments." Swing fragments are the *last* thing that you ever want to work on or think of.

Read the following statements and see how the static positions control the fragments:

1) You cannot preserve the angle unless you set the angle (position two).
2) You cannot set the angle unless you fully coil and hinge (position two).
3) You cannot finish with extension and high hands unless you preserve the angle (position two).
4) You can't fire the right side unless you load the right side by coiling (position two).
5) You can't finish facing the target with extension unless you face away from the target at position two.

Remember that the most important goal is to set up to the ball with the club face aimed at the target and the ball joined to the club's sweet spot and to return to the exact position you started from.

The obvious reason for the back-and-forth swing is to gather speed with the club so that the ball will be propelled appropriate distances. Keep that basic premise in mind and strive for consistency with the three static positions. If you become proficient at achieving consistency with these three positions, you will begin to maneuver from position to position with speed, rhythm, balance, and control.

But when the positions are "out of whack," or you get careless with them, you'll be expending energy in the wrong way—by manipulating the club with your hands in an attempt to get it back on track.

Good players don't use their hands to manipulate or force the club to stay on track. Their energy is focused on feeling the centrifugal force build and on the mental parts of the game. To play well, you no longer have to dedicate all your time to practice. Of course you must practice, but ideas on how, when, and how much you must practice have changed. Providing that you keep the *feel* of the club on a regular basis—and this doesn't necessarily require a trip to the course or driving range—you can make *major* improvement by employing these new, effective, and exciting methods.

Let's focus our attention on where the three static positions can lead us. With our minds free from thoughts of swing mechanics, we can devote our mental energies to *playing the golf course.*

5

Practice Methods

WE WILL NOW DEVOTE some time to practice methods so that you can effectively apply what you have learned and begin to groove an efficient, repeatable golf swing. We will discuss practice with regard to the three static positions and add the motion between them. The following drills combine visual confirmation of the three static positions with feel input and at the same time introduce the motion *between* the three static positions.

Static Position Drills

Now for the first drill. . . . Assume static position one in front of a mirror (see Figures 1 and 2). First check to make sure you have adequate space so as not to injure yourself or break anything. Now swing the club back to static position two (see Figures 3 and 4). Use your photographs to reinforce your drill and assist your visual con-

59

firmation in the mirror. Now swing back to position one. Repeat this process and keep moving back and forth. What you are now doing is adding the ingredient of *motion* to your static positions, motion guided by and influenced by the static positions. You will begin to feel, as you move between and to the static positions, a new freedom in your swing, a freedom only possible because of your abandoned preoccupation with separate, fragmented, piecemeal mechanics. The motion portions of your swing are now free to feel fluid, rhythmic, and empty of thought about the swing. Your *only* thought should be of your destination—the finish, the third static position. From the top, move to a correct, balanced finish, or position three (see Figures 5 and 6). Start this second drill from position two. In front of a mirror, assume a correct, balanced position two and, from there, move to the finish. Now, from the finish, move backward to position two and, while watching in the mirror, move back and forth, from position two to position three, three to two, and back again. You will feel a balanced, correct weight shift. You will feel a perfect release as you fling the ball off of the club face, and you will feel speed gather and increase as you employ centrifugal force from your motion—motion directed by the three static positions.

Now, the third drill. From position one, swing to position two. Stop a moment and swing to position three. Stop a moment at the finish, and hold your position, balanced. Now move backward to the second position, the top. Stop a moment and then move back to the finish. Now, from the finish, move to the top. Stop briefly and go back to position one. Move from position to position, back and forth, and feel the accompanying motion and how it is influenced by the quality of your balance. Balance is the steadying force in the universe. It is what fluid motion is dependent on. Lack of balance creates an immediate need for compensation, and the need for compensation takes the focus away from simple efficiency. In the golf swing, poor balance translates into jerkiness, loss of speed (due to a breakdown in the production of centrifugal force), and the need for manipulation and compensating movements, which detract from the smoothness and timing of good, effective golf swings.

When you perform these practice drills, your priority (aside from achieving the three static positions) should be to constantly keep and improve your balance. Now, armed with your photographs, your drills, your new basics (the three static positions), and your otherwise blank slate, you are ready to move farther along on our holographic journey into dimensions of golf you have never experienced. You may have had glimpses of these dimensions, maybe even extended visits, for a hole or two, but we're after bigger game. We're after consistent performance of your full potential.

I'd like to add a couple of thoughts on practice in general that I feel will expedite your improvement and help groove your golf swing.

First, in my many years of studying the golf swing, before, during and after my playing career, I have found what I feel is the most effective "training aid." It is swinging a weighted golf club. A long time ago I asked my teacher what the best exercise was for golf. I was thinking along the lines of lifting weights. He said simply, "Hitting golf balls." Of course. His answer hit me like a ton of bricks. When we swing a golf club we use a specific set of muscles. The *only* way to exercise all of those muscles at the same time is to *swing the club!* If we swing a weighted club, we are also building extra strength in those muscles. Try it on a daily basis, and you will see the improvement in your control of the golf club and hence your power.

Next I want to talk about *attitude* while practicing. If you expect to hit all good shots while practicing and you become irritated and frustrated when you don't, then you're wasting your time.

To really improve, you must learn from your bad swings and shots and use them to build improvement. You must adopt the attitude that every swing and shot, good or bad, is a step closer to a grooved, dependable technique.

Golf can easily slap you down mentally, and

the only way to steady improvement is a per-
sistently positive attitude. It is amazing how a
good shot can quickly erase the memory of a
bad one. Remember that thought, and also
remember that the most important shot in golf
is the one you're playing.

6

Shadows, Lights, and Sounds:
The Extra Input Factors

BY NOW YOUR MAIN concern should be the
quality of your three static positions, and you
should have adequate knowledge about execut-
ing them.

As you add rhythmic motion to the three positions, employing balance, acceleration through
the use of centrifugal force, and concepts such
as ball flinging, you will be "typing out" golf
shots with consistency and control. In the last
four chapters we have discussed the conventional and traditional movements and positions
that you find in golf books and magazines. By
now you should have a pretty clear vision of
your golf-swing hologram: three clear, interconnected static positions, each influencing and
influenced by the others. They are like the bird
on the credit card whose flapping wings are
frozen at different positions on the holographic

plate—positions that are all part of a flowing flight, smooth and interconnected.

Achieving consistency and quality with your three static positions takes a measure of repetitive practice, to be sure. But there are other ways to enhance and speed up your success, ways that were not known until recently, or revealed until now.

While conducting my experimental work on these new methods and concepts where I taught in Chicago and while simultaneously studying *The Holographic Universe*, I found some fascinating and functional applications to "static position enhancement." They are shadows, lights, and sounds. Remember: when the static positions are enhanced, your playing is enhanced.

Shadows

I first played golf with my dad when I was around eight or nine years old, but I think the love affair began in earnest when I was about twelve or thirteen. I can remember my early work on what right from the beginning was an art form for me. I quickly became an insatiable student of the game and spent countless hours trying everything. I tried to perfect what seemed to work and tried to purge from my technique what didn't. I still, to this day, credit my knowledge of the swing to those early study periods.

Being the creative type and having been taught good communication skills (also by my dad), it was natural that I move into the teaching arena when my best competitive days grew short. I think some of us are meant to be players forever and never teach, some are only effective at teaching, and some are lucky enough to experience both. I am thankful that I have tasted both.

Now, back to those early study periods. I used to practice in the front yard of the family home in New Orleans, which I mentally converted into a magnificent championship course. There I played with and defeated golf's legends. I copied their techniques, which I picked up on television. Some of this worked, some didn't, and there's no doubt that my early swing was a bizarre blend of movements. I also copied their rhythms and tempos, which *always* ended up being a real plus. We lived on a busy corner, and to this day, over thirty years later, my old neighbors remind me how obsessed I was with golf. I enjoyed and admired the good swings and shots just as I enjoy gazing at the works of Renoir today.

The bad swings and shots only made me work harder, and I considered each one simply another step *forward* toward my goal, a step from which to learn. At some point during one of these early days of practice, I started thinking about my shadow. I noticed that my golf swing always *felt* better when my shadow was directly over the ball. Of course, the shots were almost always better when the swing felt better. I did not give this shadow influence a great deal of thought, even though I remained very aware of it all through my early career, but there were times when I mentioned it to and tried to discuss it with friends and colleagues.

While playing on tour, I remember lying in bed one night in a motel in Natchez, Mississippi, talking with my roommate about the mysteries of life and golf until about 4:00 A.M. My roommate and traveling cohort was also one of my best friends and the number one player at Louisiana State University, Mike Keck. Mike was very cerebral and remains one of the only two or three people I've ever known who was self-actualized. Unfortunately, Mike was electrocuted at age twenty-five while trying to earn money to venture out onto the mini-tour. I'll never forget the sight of him in the casket with his Munsingwear golf shirt, Bulls Eye putter, and cocky grin. The kid would have made it big, and I really miss him. He taught me a lot during those talk sessions on the road, and I remember his thoughts about my shadow discovery, which I would bring up every so often in hopes of gleaning some insight from him. All he told me was "You'll just have to continue to explore it until it makes some kind of sense." I was always kind of disappointed that no one was ever able to help me figure out this mystery and that most people didn't even bother to give it much thought. I should stress how very important this became to me and what a strong, consistent influence it had on the quality of my swings and shots.

The simple fact of the matter is that even to this day I *almost always*, maybe 99.5 percent of the time, hit good golf shots when my shadow is over the ball. And now I'm learning why.

As time went along, it began to occur to me that the positioning and length of the shadow determined the quality and degree of its influence over my shots. I had the very best feeling when the shadow was directly over or just behind the ball and its length extended past the ball anywhere from one to four feet.

At first I came to accept the possibility that this phenomenon was just a personal thing, a quirk of some kind that gave me confidence. In other words, I couldn't figure it out, so I just went along with it, always hoping that the sun would be behind me.

As I experimented in Chicago with some of the ideas and theories formulated while studying the Holographic Principle of Interconnectedness, the long-neglected matter of trying to resolve the shadow mystery was resurrected. I played around with some ideas and then tested them on myself as well as some of my students. As I began to evolve away from traditional and conventional teaching methods, some of my students were raising eyebrows. Fortunately, the rapid and dramatic results were enough to quiet any of their questions.

There are a couple of things that I have been able to learn about "shadow positioning," and only after extensive testing have I become convinced of their merits.

FEEL INPUT

First of all, when we perform the golf swing with a ball present, we are, of course, looking at the ball. Perhaps not a specific spot, but some part of it. Staring too intently at a specific spot on the ball is very restrictive—we become "ball-bound" and lose our freedom to coil properly. Now, the fact that we are looking at the ball as we swing means that we cannot look at ourselves. The only way that we have any idea where the club is during the swing— and this is critical—is by *feeling* where it is. It is the only input that we have to discern club location. I call this input our "feel input."

Our sense of timing is made apparent to us by the feel input, and our sense of position (where we are and where the club is) is also fed to us by this "feel."

VISUAL INPUT

What I have discovered, however, is that when the sun is *directly* behind us our shadow is projected out over the area where the ball lies and becomes visible during the setup and swing. We certainly don't consciously look at our shadow as we swing, but we do *see* it as we swing (Figure 9). Being able to see the shadow of our setup and swing *as we perform the swing* gives us another input, a "visual input" to go along with our feel input, and this can promote some very positive influences on the quality of our performance.

Figure 9: The shadow as visual imput.

First of all, "seeing" ourselves as we swing enables us to monitor our technique and make adjustments. Without visual input we simply have to trust, by feel alone, that the club and our body are in position. To test how effective visual input can be, just swing for a while in front of a mirror. When swinging in front of a mirror, you can adjust your positions and make better swings.

Second, and possibly most important, visual input gives us an accurate and direct awareness of our rhythm and tempo. We can see where the club is and where our body is. Being able to see our swing speed helps us *control* that speed. One of golf's most damaging and universal errors is the tendency to rush back to the ball. Players swing back too fast, fail to get set at the top, and then rush back to hit the ball. The main cause of rushing is a player's inability to know where the club is. Without the confidence of controlling the club, the "hit-the-ball" urge takes over, prompting the hands and arms to make a fast swipe at it.

I have had amazing results with the visible input idea. Often I watch students hit one poor shot after another in total frustration, and then move them to a location where the sun is behind them. I then let them hit a few shots before instructing them to be aware of their shadow as they setup and swing. I have had incredible results with this method, and it works quickly for everyone. I want to stress, though, that the shadow must be either directly over or slightly behind the ball, and it must be elongated enough to extend at least one-to-four feet beyond the ball, that is, directly in front of you at a right angle to the target line.

Obviously, this exact positioning does not take place very often and that is what gave me fits early on, when I was not inclined to delve into the mystery very deeply. But now that I have, I have found ways to take advantage of this extremely effective influence.

First of all, I tell my students to try to practice where the shadow can be positioned properly. Many times this is not easily accomplished. If the sun is out, but you just cannot (for logistical reasons) get properly positioned, then I would have you at least take lots of practice swings with the shadow in position. Sometimes the sun will not even be available, and then, clearly, you can't do anything with your shadow. But this method is so effective and so important that I have even used a photographer's lamp to produce the shadow on cloudy days.

The bottom line is this: when you swing with the advantage of extra input factors—feel input and visual input—you swing better. The more repetitions you perform using these positive influences, the more correct muscle memory you build. Even without a ball, the frequent correct repetition will eventually become your technique. For those of you who benefit immediately from the use of the shadow, I'd like to share a technique which can enhance your usage of this effective extra input factor. I have found that by using imagery, it is possible to call up your

shadow anytime, anywhere. You've got to practice it often and conscientiously, but if you do,
you will see that you can stand up to the ball on a
cloudy day and see your shadow out over the
ball. With some practice and imagination, the
mind's eye can see with amazing clarity.

Lights

Darkness is a void. Light connotes energy. It is
well known that people (and many animals) are
more productive, energetic, and happy on
bright, sunny days. While dreary, cloudy days
are a depressant to most people, brightness
makes us vibrant and alert. Think of every picture you've ever seen of Las Vegas on the strip
where the millions of bright and blinking lights
make the picture come *alive* with activity. You
can give your golf game a positive charge of
energy by using imaginary lights. When you
use imagery, you do two things: you incorporate positive thoughts and by doing so you
squeeze out and replace negative thoughts with
positive ones. For example, you're standing on
the tee of a long par four with water on the left
and out of bounds on the right. A large, deep
fairway bunker guards the right side of the fairway. If you ask most players what they are
thinking of as they prepare to drive the ball,
you'll get answers like these: (1) "Don't hook it
into the lake," (2) "Don't push it too far right in

avoiding the water," and (3) "Steer away from the fairway bunker."

Only really good players will answer with "I see a little area in the left center of the fairway that would leave me with perfect position. I'll aim my drive there and hit it there."

Really good players can think that way because they're good enough to consistently hit the ball where they aim it. Most players, however, need help. Most players are so unsure of their technique that they can't confidently stand on that tee and disregard all of the trouble that lurks. These players need the benefits that imagery can bring.

Light Imagery

I've found that seeing and feeling light can give the body energy, and thinking of or imagining light can give the *mind* energy. I call it "light imagery."

Again, I want to stress that just as you must practice your chip shots over and over again until you become confident, you must practice imagery over and over again until it becomes clear and real. The more real it becomes, the more effect it has on your muscle movement.

Now you're back on that tee, standing behind the ball, looking at the layout of the hole. Using imagery, I want you to visualize the fairway as a runway, a runway with bordering lights. Bright, blinking lights line the fairway on either side. Look down this runway to your desired landing area and see a tall, very bright stadium light. Aim your shot down this runway at the tall light and then go into your routine and swing. With practice, you'll be amazed at how the tension leaves your thoughts and your swing. It's all because you've focused *away* from dark negative factors and focused directly *on* positive, energetic objectives.

When playing shots to the green, visualize the entire green as an arena, bursting with light and crowds. (When using imagery and visualization, use detail.) Once you can actually "see" the arena, picture the flagstick as its center, and then send your shot into the arena, into its center.

By employing these visualization methods, you take the focus away from the negative possibilities and place it on new, nonpenalizing objectives. Using lights brings a dimension of energy into the equation. The bottom line is that lights make us feel happy, energetic, and excited in a calm, positive way. To experience this, just walk out of your front door on a crisp, bright spring day with the sun bathing everything with its light and warmth and compare that feeling to waking up on a cold, dark, rainy morning when you've got eight appointments. Light, when used in positive visualization, can be another factor that you can add to your arsenal against negative thinking.

Sounds

Another important sensory perception that can add yet another valuable input factor to your practice and your playing is the "sound of golf." In *Golf in the Kingdom,* Shivas Irons says to *listen* to the sounds of the golf course and to the sounds of your foursome. He asks Michael to replace negative thoughts with diverse, serene, calming sounds: wind blowing through trees, leaves rustling, birds chirping. But even faraway sounds like trains, boats, planes and traffic will be apparent to you once you learn to really listen to the sounds of golf. You'll find the sounds of your foursome truly remarkable and unending.

Even more valuable is the sound of your own shots and swing. Listen to the sounds that good players produce when practicing (the sounds of impact). These can have positive effects on your game. There is a practice tool that I have been using with some students that makes good use of the sounds of golf. I tell students who are lacking in the distance department to swing the club and listen to the sound, the "swish" that the club makes as it moves through the hitting area (impact zone). When they hear the swish, I tell them to make it *louder* on the next swing. Of course, what makes the "swish" louder is retaining the ninety-degree angle farther into the down-swing and then fully opening it at impact. As the player attempts to make a louder swish, he is automatically delaying this angle and then releasing it quickly and completely.

It is something you can practice without a ball and without a practice range, and the beauty of it is that as the swish gets louder, the club-head speed increases and the ball goes farther. Sound is just another valuable input factor that gives you a positive influence to tap into and enhance your feel. When we make full use of our senses, our minds have more ammunition with which to influence the movements of our muscles.

Aside from the positive physical effects that these input factors produce, they also leave less room and time for negative thoughts. And some, like listening to the sounds of the golf course, can keep us calm and tension-free.

An Anatomical Gift

In 1992, the U.S. Women's Amateur Championship was played at Kemper Lakes Golf Club in Chicago.

I was asked to play along during a practice round by two of Illinois' best young players, Marla Jemsek (the daughter of Frank Jemsek of Coghill) and Nicole Jeray, on the day before the qualifying round. We teed off at about 7:00 A.M. with the ground blanketed by dew, so much so that it looked like snow covered the golf course.

On the third hole, a par four of about 370 yards, I hit a pitching wedge second shot to the green and then proceeded to walk on up to the green to mark and clean my ball. While watching one of the other players pitch to the green, I happened to look back at my "tracks" leading to the green. I had walked a straight line about 100 yards and the footsteps were most vivid because of the dew. I noticed something that I had never noticed before: when I walk, my left foot steps straight ahead but my right foot points "out" or to the right about 20 degrees. For most of my career my golf stance has been the opposite of that "natural," anatomical foot placement. I have always placed my right foot pretty much perpendicular to the target line and my left foot splayed out somewhat.

The next day on the practice tee at Ruffled Feathers, a wonderful new Pete Dye layout in Lemont, I experimented with my stance and hit some shots with my feet in their "natural" position. The results were astounding. I was striking the ball extremely well and, more important, felt comfortable as I did so. The "natural" stance seemed to facilitate a more efficient coil on the backswing, and offered stability and proper resistance through the swing. In the months that followed, I experimented with students, first determining their natural position, and then having them stand that way to swing. The results were uniformly positive.

In golf, you must go with nature, not against it. You must let your anatomy become an *ally*, not a complication. When you walk, the position your feet are in is your natural stance; any other foot position is unnatural, and goes against the grain of your physical make-up. I'm passing this "anatomical gift" on to you, and urge you to walk through the dew to discover *your* natural stance. You will love the results.

7

Mirrors

MIRRORS HAVE BEEN greatly overlooked and neglected as an aid in practicing, perfecting, and grooving the golf swing. I would personally say that aside from my front-yard practice as a youngster, mirrors probably had the second-greatest influence on my technique. I believe that from a tempo standpoint, mirrors had the single greatest positive effect. Like the shadow, the mirror gives us *visual* input as we attempt to feel our way through the golf swing. The big difference is that when using the mirror, we look into it instead of down at the ball. As we shall see, however, in some ways the work with mirrors is more effective. One great advantage is that we can practice in front of a mirror in cold, rain, or snow, and we don't have to drive anywhere to do it. I believe that this practice method is so important that I prescribe it for *every* student with whom I work, regardless of ability.

First of all, let's discuss what kind of mirror you'll need to work with for maximum benefit. You want a mirror that allows you to see your entire swing, and you want one that does not distort the image. These are the two criteria. You also want to place the mirror in a space that does not restrict your ability to swing freely or where damage could occur to your surroundings or to other individuals. Using a mirror is a great way to check your three static positions for form and correct positioning. It enables you to see your positions *with motion* without using a still or video camera.

I started discovering the benefits of working with mirrors during my first assistant pro position at Lakewood Country Club in New Orleans. The golf shop at Lakewood had this wonderfully large mirror on one wall, and the shop just happened to have ceilings that were about twenty feet high.

Lakewood Country Club in those days (1967) only had about 300 members, but it was the home course of a PGA Tour event—the New Orleans Open. Most of the other fifty-one weeks of the year were comparatively boring, so naturally I had plenty of time to practice, play, tinker with clubs, and experiment. Fortunately, my boss, head professional Jim Hart, encouraged my self-development. Jim is not in the golf business anymore, but I always had a lot of respect for his professionalism and knowledge of the golf swing. He was (and still is) a fine player. Anyway, I would spend *countless* hours swinging in front of that mirror, and I found that by watching myself as I swung, I could make instant corrections to movements and positions. I would make a change, confirm its correctness in the mirror, and then perform my readjusted swing over and over again in front of the mirror. It was like hitting balls but better because I could *see* whether or not I was swinging the way I wanted to. If I swung enough times in front of the mirror, I would usually be able to duplicate this movement on the practice tee because I had grooved my swing in front of the mirror by numerous repetitions, all the while having instant visual confirmation of the quality of the swings. I also found that by watching my swing as I performed it, I could directly control the tempo—the speed and rhythm of my acceleration.

You might hit two hundred balls on the practice range trying to perfect a specific aspect of your swing, but the only feedback that you have is how it *feels*. With the mirror, you can feel it while you *see* it.

Sight and Feel Method

It is no wonder that years later, when I played on the PGA Tour, I saw players swinging and setting up in front of the mirrors in their motel rooms. I learned that this is the best way to piece your swing together or to incorporate something new into an existing swing. I call it the Sight and Feel Method. Let me give you an example of how it works.

Let's say you want to work on your position at the top, static position number two. You assume your address position (static position number one) in front of the mirror and swing to the second static position while watching your swing. Make any necessary changes and repeat your swing until you're satisfied with your position at the top. While watching in the mirror, continue to repeat it until you can consistently put the club where you want it.

Now, set up again in front of the mirror, but this time don't look at yourself while you swing. Swing to the top, stop, hold your position, and then look into the mirror to see if it matches the position you achieved while watching. Repeat this process enough times and you will soon be able to match positions. This works amazingly well and much faster than if you just hit ball after ball on the practice tee, not knowing for sure if you're achieving the position you're trying to reach.

This instant visual confirmation and visual image feedback method is a very powerful and effective way to work on the three static positions and the resultant motional movements.

Another valuable asset of this method is that

you can check things out from different angles. You can stand in different positions and see the plane of your swing, the width of your arc, and your degree of weight shift. Most important, however, is that you can work on your three static positions with immediate feedback. You can stop your swing at any point (since you're not swinging at a ball) and see how the motion parts of your swing are being influenced by the static positions. Corrections can be made immediately, confirmed visually, and then incorporated into your technique using the Sight and Feel Method of mirror practice.

Tempo

Since swinging in front of a mirror is the best way I've found for working on tempo, I think that we should, at this point, expand on tempo and see how it is enhanced by mirror work.

When people comment on a good, effective golf swing, saying how effortless and rhythmic it appears, what they're really seeing and saying is that the swing has a good tempo, or pace.

Let me try to define what constitutes good tempo in a good golf swing. The best way to describe it is to say that the club head moves from start to finish without any jerkiness. It moves *smoothly* and unhurriedly to the second static position, and when it begins its motion to the area where the ball lies, it moves with *gradual, but constant* acceleration, reaching maximum speed in the immediate area of the ball. A characteristic of poor swings is that the club head often *decelerates* as it approaches the ball, a result of a dissipation of the energy stored in the left-arm-club-shaft angle and a failure to generate centrifugal force. Another characteristic of a poor golf swing is a rushed backswing, failure to *set* the second static position and a rushed attempt to get back to the ball. Usually the player overuses the hands in such a swing with little buildup of centrifugal force. Study the swings of good players and see how they swing the club back slowly and smoothly, set at the top, and then accelerate to the ball. Good players know that you don't contact the ball during the backswing—they are in no particular hurry.

Swinging in front of a mirror affords you the opportunity to *see* the speed of your swing, as well as feel it. While looking into the mirror, set up in static position one and swing slowly to the top, set the position, then accelerate to the third position. Adding this visual element to your practice lets you simultaneously combine the two things you need to practice and at the same time receive instant confirmation of the quality of your practice. These two things are (1) repetition of the fundamentally sound three static positions and (2) free motion with a regulated tempo.

As you practice in front of the mirror, swinging while watching, alternate watching yourself with watching the spot where a ball would be. This does two things. It gets you used to having your head in the normal playing position, and teaches you the feeling of a free swing and body turn, feelings that being ball-bound can destroy. This added input factor has so many benefits that it is impossible to overstate its value.

Calling It Up

Just as you can "call up" the shadow over the ball, so can you, with practice, call up or visualize the mirror in front of you. You can become so effective at this form of visualization that you can actually "see" your swing in the mirror. Again, the point of these visualization techniques is that *the more good swings you make, with or without a ball, the more your swing becomes grooved and will eventually override your poor swing habits and become your technique.*

The shadow and the mirror are two tremendously effective ways to get you to make good swings because you're not relying simply on where you *think* you feel the club.

The Swing Plane

Using a mirror is a great way to work on or check your swing plane, which is one of the most overlooked and important properties of an effective golf swing. The arc of the swing is the path the club head makes as it moves around the body. A wide arc means that the circle around the body made by the club head is as far from the body as possible. This, as we now know, is achieved by maintaining an extended left arm from address to well after impact. The *plane* of the swing is the degree to which the arc is vertical or horizontal. The common terms describing swing plane, the terms you hear most frequently, are "flat" and "upright."

A flat swing plane is more horizontal to the ground and happens when the club-head arc moves *inside* the target line rather abruptly as it moves away from the ball.

An upright swing plane is more vertical to the ground and occurs when the club-head arc moves *along* the target line for a longer period of time as it moves away from the ball. If you address the ball in a mirror to your right (mirror facing parallel to the target line), you will be able to see your swing plane. When practicing or altering your swing plane, use the Sight and Feel Method of mirror practice for quick results and a precise reading to check it. The swing plane that is most effective for you depends on your anatomical makeup and your address position, including posture and distance from the ball.

A consistently applicable rule, however, is that a swing plane that is too flat or too upright will make it difficult to achieve optimum results with your technique.

Don't underestimate the value of mirror practice because, like the shadow, it gives you added input as you work on your technique. Use of this added input can accelerate the development of your golf swing.

8

Playing the Game Holographically

IN THIS CHAPTER we will move from the mechanical side of the game to the holographic side. Of course, swing mechanics always require attention and repetitive practice, but the other side must be given equal attention. This other side, the side we'll call "strategic," involves taking our golf swing (with its ball-flinging capabilities) and moving the golf ball around the course with maximum efficiency, taking advantage of all "helping currents" available. These helping currents include wind, terrain, atmospheric conditions, and our own considerable mental energies.

Taking into account the Holographic Principle of Interconnectedness, we can fuse the golf swing, the ball, and the golf course into a melody of maximum performance. Negotiating the course in the fewest strokes possible is the object of the game, and just striking the ball well does not ensure that objective. We will come to see that the mechanical side of golf and the strategic side can greatly influence one another, and your ability to reach your *full* potential can only occur when the proper mix is achieved.

How We Perceive the Golf Course

Most golfers, when the time comes to play, view the golf course as a minefield of trouble, seeing only bunkers, roughs, lakes, out-of-bounds, and dense trees as places to avoid. But the very same golfer who dwells on these trouble spots may later see the course quite differently from the clubhouse window at sunset. It then becomes a beautiful, serene place with natural beauty, birds, and a generally calming quality. How often have I seen harried executives arrive at the course for an afternoon of relaxation and cama- raderie, only to head home hours later more frustrated and angry than when they left the office! The game's ability to affect us that way is at the heart of what makes low scoring so diffi- cult. The fact is, most golfers fight the game and fight the course rather than recognize that there are "helping currents," as Shivas Irons says, everywhere. Golfers commonly complain around clubhouses and in locker rooms about "hitting the ball great" on the practice range and then *playing* poorly when it counts. Something happens on the way from the penalty-free practice tee to the mine-filled golf course.

Fear of the golf course is propagated by a preoccupation with mechanical technique. But, in truth, every technique, no matter how well developed, contains flaws and will produce a certain number of poor swings. But these imperfect performances can be held to their natural minimum by eliminating negative thoughts and fears. When these negative factors are given free rein, the mind sends uncertain messages and directions to the muscles, which react with increased tension and tentativeness. In previous chapters we touched on how imagery, visualization, and positive-thought replacement can ward off and minimize the effects of these negative thoughts and influences, but there are more steps available to us. One of the main reasons that golf can be so frustrating and evoke such anger lies in the very nature of the game. Golf is a solitary game that involves no teammates to lean on or fault. We have only ourselves to blame and only ourselves for support. It is easy to blame ourselves, especially when we find that "ourselves" aren't strong enough to lean on. Golf lays us bare, exposes our deeper selves, and brings our darker side closer to the surface. There is nowhere to hide when we seek to escape our own exposed inadequacies. We almost always play golf with other people, but we play totally *alone*. And just notice, when you play alone, how much more accepting you are of poor shots and missed putts. Notice how well your self-anger is controlled when playing alone because your ineptness is not evident to the discerning and critical eyes of others. It is the apprehension of possibly being exposed as inadequate that brings the fear to the surface, and then the fear, like a cancer, multiplies and devours the healthy positive feelings. By learning to use every available positive tool, the focus of this chapter, we can shrink the cancer of fear and play the course the same way we play the practice tee, with a relaxed confidence free of penalties. Only then can we reach our full potential and enjoy the art of golf.

Some years ago several top players were asked what they saw and thought of when standing on the tee of a hole with out-of-bounds to the left, a lake to the right, and fairway bunkers dotting both sides of the fairway. The players gave answers like "I tend to draw the ball, so I'll try to keep it a little to the right" (to avoid the out-of-bounds) or "I tend to fade the ball, so I'll try to aim a little farther left" (to avoid the lake), and so on. When the question was posed to Ben Hogan, he said, "I'm aiming at and thinking of a thirty-foot-diameter circle where I'd like the ball to finish." It is no wonder that Hogan was regarded as having intense and pure concentration, and it is no wonder that he is widely regarded as the most accurate controller of the golf ball who ever played. As we learned earlier, concentration is born out of a consistent routine which you develop through practice. But the most rigid and disciplined routine can be blown apart by not handling potential stumbling blocks properly. Would Hogan have emerged as the game's leading practitioner of concentration had he dwelt on lakes, bunkers, and out-of-bounds stakes? Of course not. Hogan *used* the positive locations and influences to enhance his ability, not the negative ones to tear that ability down.

Positive Locations

For every trouble spot on a golf course there are a thousand positive locations. Try this experiment sometime: set aside a couple of hours one day and walk around your (or any) golf course *without playing*. Stand on the tee and survey each hole. You'll be surprised to see, once free from the pressures of playing, how docile and beautiful the course is under these conditions, when only hours ago it was a demon with pitfalls at every turn. Take the time to walk the holes, all of them. As you walk the holes, you'll be surprised to see how much "safe room" there is on each one, regardless of how intimidating the hole may appear when you play it with the pressure of scoring on your mind (Figure 10).

Figure 10: Positive locations

I first noticed the positive effects of this when I played on the PGA Tour and had to scout new courses that I'd never laid eyes on before. I realized that there was a lot more room for error on the course than I thought. That realization took some of the pressure off, and reduced any tendency to "steer" the ball away from trouble. As you walk your course, your first job is to survey the teeing area and how it aligns with the layout of the hole. Many tee boxes (teeing areas) are in straight alignment with trouble spots such as trees, rough, or water hazards. Unfortunately, very few are aligned with positive locations.

We define "positive location" as a place away from trouble spots which affords easy and clear access to the next positive location. High-level golf involves moving the ball around the course from one positive location to another. Aligning your body with the tee box does not assure you of being lined up with the location where you'd like the ball to finish.

After checking the tee's alignment, the next consideration is choosing the desired landing area, or positive location, for the first shot of the hole. When you walk the hole, you will be able to check out the best spot from which to play your second shot. Obviously, on most par-three holes your initial stroke is played to the green. Even so, *what part* of the green you aim for is important, given considerations such as pin position and trouble areas. When you consider your positive locations, give careful thought to planning the safest and most effective way to get to them. For instance, let's say that your positive location is on the right side of the fairway and there are fairway bunkers and an out-of-bounds down the left side. To the right is only light rough. There is no wind to speak of, and you consistently fade the ball slightly. The right side is your positive location, with the area further to the right the next most strategically safe choice. All of the serious trouble is to the left. The most logical plan of attack is to attempt to start the ball at the right edge of the fairway bunkers on the left and let the expected fade take the ball to your chosen positive location. If the wind is blowing right to left, your aim should be directly at your chosen spot so that the wind will cancel out your fade and result in a straight trajectory. If the wind is blowing left to right, then perhaps you will want to start the shot *at* the fairway bunkers and let your ball "ride the wind" back to the right toward your objective. Whenever possible, try to ride the wind or let it help your shot, rather than fight against it. If you are accomplished enough as a player to be able to "work the ball" left to right, right to left, and high and low, then you can take great advantage of the wind and make it an ally. Take great care in determining the wind direction and its velocity. Then you will know just what effect it will have on any given shot. Try to remember that even when the wind is directly in your face, a solid, well-struck shot will not be affected as much as you think. One of the main causes of loss of balance during the golf swing is trying to swing too hard, especially when playing directly into the wind. As you walk the golf course, make charts and notes of positive locations along each hole, including the teeing areas and greens. Looking at these notes and charts later will not only get you focused on positive locations, but will trigger the memory of walking the hole so you'll remember how much safe room there really is. This is another positive calming influence.

We just mentioned how wind currents can help you find positive locations for your shots. Another aid is the course itself, specifically the terrain. Slopes, hills, mounds, swales, and different types of grass can all influence your golf shots, both negatively and positively. When looking at a golf hole, try to see its general view, the total layout of the terrain. Some golf-course architects are master illusionists who can make a golf course *look* much harder than it really is. Many holes appear to be extremely difficult from the tee but are actually not difficult at all once you've walked the hole and seen how much safe room is out there. One of the trademarks of Pete Dye, who is certainly one of the world's leading course designers, is his ability to create an illusion of difficulty. One of my favorite Pete Dye designs, the Old Marsh Club in West Palm Beach, Florida, will scare you to death standing on the tees, but it actually affords lots of room in the desired landing areas.

The Secret of Scoring

Here's a tip for avoiding disaster on the golf course: when you walk and chart your positive locations for your shots, seek out the *center* of your safe landing area. Get a fix on these spots and learn how to aim at them as you play. This will give you *plenty* of room for error and is much more effective than just "aiming down the fairway." Remember, the secret to scoring in golf is "how good your bad shots are." If you constantly aim at the center of positive locations, you will minimize the penalty shots, the "disasters." Avoiding the double bogeys and worse is the key to scoring. Golf should be played like a chess match or billiards, not like a free-swinging home-run derby.

Golf and Interconnectedness

The golf ball, the club, the swing, and the golf course must be enjoined in the performance of playing. It is ineffective and self-defeating to play golf with the notion of hitting a golf ball with a club and overpowering the golf course. Careful planning *must* be involved. Good players never slash their way around the course. They take their three static positions, along with the feeling of ball flinging, and fling the ball around the course, from one positive location to another, taking advantage of any helping current available, whether it be wind, terrain, or anything else that can ease the path. They use visualization and imagery, positive-thought replacement, blending, even sounds, to enhance or produce their best efforts. I've known players who use melodies to establish their rhythms and cadences while setting up and swinging.

The point is, every positive influence available should be discovered and used *in conjunction* with the actual swing. This is the essence of Holographic Golf. Just as a hologram of a bird (when viewed from several angles) creates the illusion of soaring without showing the actual mechanics of each wing movement, the three static positions create the illusion of a complete swing without showing the many positions in between.

What Concentration Really Is

People miss eighteen-inch putts and walk off of the green saying, "I just didn't concentrate." Concentration doesn't just happen automatically. Concentration must be practiced, just like the three static positions. Concentration comes from having a plan, a plan made up of positive thoughts, routines, and visualizations. When your mind is occupied with positive thoughts and attitudes to the point that it is "filled up," there is no room for negatives. When you've reached that point, you've got pure concentration. Concentration takes discipline and practice, and it can be cultivated to an amazingly high degree of intensity and effectiveness.

Touring pros have for years been accused of being "robots": colorless, emotionless, and boring. Well, so are chess masters, billiard champions, and poets. Things that require intense concentration leave little room for outward displays of gaiety, because concentration requires all your attention on the *routine*. Even if you're a thirty handicapper, paying close attention to this "other" side of golf, the nonmechanical side, will lower your score more quickly and drastically than twenty lessons on swing mechanics.

9

Farther Down the Fairways

WHERE HAS GOLF come since the invention of the steel shaft? If you measure in terms of numbers of great players on the PGA Tour, it's come a long way. Why are there more good players at the top levels of the game? There is one answer, and only one. As prize money has escalated, *greater numbers* of young golfers seriously pursue the game.

Instruction, until now, has not accounted for very much improvement for the average golfer, simply because instruction has been mired in a state of stagnation. The truth is, instructors the world over have nowhere to turn except to electronic innovations, and these pathetic gimmicks are now more abundant than ever. The trade magazines and their instructional pieces have been saying the same things for thirty years, with different people taking turns changing the words and phrases. Let's return to the question that began this chapter, but this time let's ask it in terms of the golfing masses. Since the invention of the steel shaft, how far have the golfing masses come in terms of improvement?

Let's let the statistics of the National Golf Foundation answer for us: they've come nowhere. Still, after all these years of advice from the "experts" and with all of the technological advances in equipment, not to mention the superb conditioning of golf courses, the golfing masses have trouble breaking one hundred. Friends, something has been wrong. With this book we can begin to focus on the things that *will* bring the scores down—finally. The way down is through the three static positions and attention to the other side of the game, the side that Shivas Irons teaches. That other side of golf, the nonmechanical side, is not just "good reading." It is very real, and it is very much *the way* toward mechanical proficiency. Since my involvement with the other side of golf and my growing study and application of the Holographic Principle of Interconnectedness of all things, my teaching practice has delivered spectacular results with *all* students, and I am just scratching the surface. The potential impact of my new method on the world of instruction is exciting, to say the least. I'd like to give you a glimpse of what may lie farther down the fairways.

As scientists the world over inch closer to finding the bridge between mind and matter (read *Synchronicity* by F. David Peat), human performance will find its source in the far regions of the mind, regions that for so long have been misused or unused. For a glimpse of the power the mind has over the body, let's look at the players who had a special gift:

There was Hogan, whose purity of concentration made him the game's consummate robot, with ball-striking precision that became legend, especially among his peers.

Then there was Arnold Palmer, whose confidence and determination led to exploits on the golf courses of the world that literally transformed the game to the high social level it now occupies. Nearly two decades of *special* excellence were splashed worldwide by the media with accounts of Palmer "willing" the ball into the hole.

Next came Jack Nicklaus, who is unquestionably the greatest golfer of all time. Nicklaus, through his powers of imagery and visualization and his combination of will, intellect, and concentration, achieved a physical excellence unmatched by anyone.

There have been others who have displayed similar traits and achieved high levels of excellence: Gary Player, Raymond Floyd, Lee Trevino, and Byron Nelson, to name just a few.

The Zone

Whenever any of these great players was performing his special artistry, he was said to have been in "The Zone." What is this Zone? How do you get there? And what lies beyond?

All of us, regardless of skill level, have glimpsed the zone—that string of good shots, the consecutive birdies, the hot putting round, the best score ever. When we're in the zone, we are on that bridge between mind and matter. When we find ourselves there, for a brief time our muscles receive *clear* and *unaltered* directives from the mind. During a poor performance the directives are not clear; they are prejudiced and altered by negative thoughts, self-doubts, and knowledge of past failures. But every now and then, just as with the seemingly random appearances of synchronicities, we stumble onto that bridge and the link between thought and action is positive and productive. The truly great performers all seem to have highly developed abilities of concentration, which seems to be one of the keys that unlocks the door to the zone.

Worth mentioning at this point is a much overlooked fact about the great players and their greatest achievements. They always take place in front of large galleries, often numbering up to twenty thousand. Somehow, the special players feed off of the energy of their highly focused, nearly silent spectators. The human energy involved is enormous, and this energy flows between the player and the crowd. The closest I ever came to feeling it was in the early

1970s. I was paired a couple of groups ahead of Arnold Palmer at Rio Pinar Country Club in Orlando, Florida. At every green there was a throng anxiously awaiting the arrival of the of the "king." On about the seventh or eighth hole, a par five, I hit my third shot, a three-quarter wedge, six feet behind the hole, and it spun back to within six inches of the cup. The crowd of about five thousand exploded into applause. It was the first time that had ever happened to me, and I can tell you that every hair on my body stood up with a rush of adrenaline and a feeling of electricity. Can you imagine playing *every* shot of your career with *that* potential on every shot? It's enough to put you in the zone and keep you there!

It is said that all of us have energy fields around us. This is a fact. Our brain waves are electrical in nature, and they can be measured and monitored. "Special" people, people who are considered the best at what they do—world leaders, charismatic people and performers, famous people, gifted athletes—all have highly developed "energy fields," and many people claim to be able to see that energy field in the form of auras. Shivas Irons and Seamus Mac-Duff called it the *inner body,* or the *luminous body,* and there is exhaustive scientific evidence that this inner body does exist in all of us. As you read *Golf in the Kingdom* and *The Holographic Universe,* you will learn much more about this important other part of yourself. Learn as much as you can about your inner body, because it will be an important ally as you move farther down the fairways.

True Gravity

To quote Shivas Irons, "True gravity, 'tis Seamus' term for the deeper lines o' force, the deeper structure of the universe." Today's scientists who are studying subjects like the Holographic Principle of Interconnectedness and synchronicities call it the *implicate* order, or the *enfolded* order. These theories involve everything in the universe being interconnected and ordered, with no such things as coincidence, randomness, chance, or luck. Shivas says that you can only know true gravity by "livin' into it yer'sel'—ye must go into the heart o' it, through yer own body and senses and livin' experience, level after level right to the heart o' it." Shivas is talking about the other side of golf (and life), of knowing it from *within*. The three static positions are the most *conscious* of your methods, the way to *mechanical* repetitiveness and efficiency. But they will not really stick unless you can successfully call them up, and that is what the other side of golf is about: it's to evoke, out of the implicate order, the inner body's ability to get the fibers of our muscles to perform, in true gravity, the three static positions and resultant effective motions.

From *Golf in the Kingdom*

"There are other terms in Shivas Irons' vocabulary roughly synonymous with 'True Gravity,' such as 'feeling-force' and 'heart power.' Gravity as described by Sir Isaac Newton is a concept rendered with mathematical equations which are used to achieve certain feats of prediction and control in the physical sphere. 'True gravity' connotates force, but it is also a highly aware entering and joining of those 'swarming fields' that make up our universe.* It would bring our overcontrolling manipulative ways back into harmony with nature on all its levels, animate and inanimate. It is good for man to assume power, but power joined to consciousness (as Pythagoras had intended)."

Streamers of Heart Power

In the 1960s, millions of people were caught up in the excitement created by Arnold Palmer. Almost every media account of Palmer's amazing rallies included a description of his apparent ability to will the ball to the intended target. Palmer, during those times, could stand over the ball and see the line over which he wanted the ball to roll or fly.

---

*When Arnold Palmer was performing his magic and willing the ball into the hole while trapping millions in his web of charisma, when Jack Nicklaus was *consistently* birdieing tough holes under pressure, when Hogan walked to the winner's circle in a trance,

Haven't you had the experience of seeing the line of a putt and then have the ball follow that line into the hole? I know I have and everyone I know who has played the game has experienced it. But, this has happened to most of us only on *rare* occasions, and try as we might, we can't call this ability up at will. To people like Arnold Palmer and Jack Nicklaus though, this occurrence happens almost daily. At this point, I'd like to quote several paragraphs from *Golf in the Kingdom*, from a passage subtitled "Visualizing the Ball's Flight: How images become irresistible paths" (Figure 11):

When Shivas told me the story of his conversion (to an awareness of an inner world), he said that his

---

they were all in the zone, they were playing golf in "true gravity." The mechanical, outward side of their games was but a manifestation of their *inner state*, the purity of concentration that transports the mind to true gravity. When the mind can operate with such focused clarity, the body receives its clearest signal and performs accordingly. This state can be cultivated and perfected, and it begins, as we learned earlier, with consistent routine. It is also nurtured by having a mind uncluttered by confusion and negative thoughts. The three static positions will erase the mechanical clutter, and the blending, visualization, and thought replacement will squeeze out the negative thoughts, and then, with repetitive practice of *both* sides of the game, the visits into true gravity will become more frequent.

obsession with epilepsy and dismemberment was a "prophetic image," a "psychic body" as real as any body we can see. It had emerged from the unconscious, he said, with a power to transform. Such visitations may come to us all at crucial moments of change in our lives. But we do not have to wait passively for their coming; we can deliberately cultivate them to support a discipline, or help us hit a golf shot. I have already discussed the value of negative thoughts like the one that was telling me to straighten out my life: by letting that voice speak to me clearly, I learned a valuable lesson. Shivas did the same kind of thing when the image of epilepsy exploded in his inner eye and he fell into the ecstatic state that changed his life forever. In both cases the "prophetic image" had to be recognized and accepted before it could do its work.

But images that we *deliberately* foster without any obsessive inward leading can also have a transforming power. [This is why "calling up your shadow" works!] Meditation on a golf ball may help you get a sense of life's wholeness, for a sphere is an archetype of perfection (Parmenides thought being itself was a globe); or contemplating its diminutive size, the fact that it weighs just an ounce and a half, may lead you to see that in some sense this world is light as a feather, that all life is, as Shivas said, "an earthy nothingness." In his journal he had written that meditation is an art we need—we lose our way so easily in this teeming world, with eyes open and with eyes closed, on prophetic images and the consequences of our acts, until true gravity takes us up. Along with our inward turnings he would have us stay open to all around us, including the disarray our acts so often bring. On a golf course he was insistent that we follow the flight of every shot to the very end—no matter how bad that shot may be. That is the only way to learn from our mistakes and our successes. It is the only way our unconscious mind can absorb the information it is given; and "we blind ourselves by turning away too soon." (What lessons there are for the rest of our life!) But the most basic kind of meditation during a round of golf is the visualization of our shot as we stand up to the ball. An image in our mind can become an irresistible path. Many players will tell you they often see their shot before they make it. Many well-

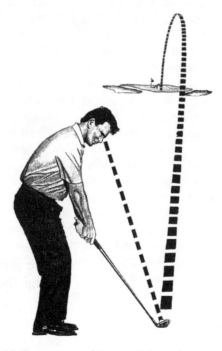

Figure 11: Imagery and irresistible paths.

known teachers recommend visualization as one of the game's most important secrets. Shivas said that as you practiced this skill of the inner eye, you would develop a capacity which put forth "Streamers of Heart Power for the ball to fly on." At times it has seemed that my mental picture has changed the direction of a shot after it has left the ground, as if I were steering it from afar. But those living and tangible images cannot be forced by brute will. Sometimes they form themselves as if guided by a superior intelligence. Whether or not these "Streamers" are real remains a question you will have to decide for yourself. They are certainly real in *some* sense. Reality as we ordinarily perceive it is much less rigid than our recent past has taught us.

Now let's move farther down the fairways for a glimpse at what the future holds for the game and those who love to play it. Golf, with its endless applications pertinent to the philosophies of life and its setting in nature so conducive to such a shrinelike atmosphere, will become like a religion and will be a mandatory part of every child's "learning repertoire." The courses themselves will be temples of instruction, with lessons learned at every turn.

Instructors will become even more gurulike, with many Shivas Irons types leading the way. The trade magazines, instead of trying to tell you how to "delay the hands on the downswing" in their monthly tips, will be telling you about true gravity or blending or will feature methods of visualization. Equipment, because of the USGA's stringent (and fortunate) control, will remain largely unchanged save for the attention to individuality with regard to custom specifications and appearance. It is a good thing for the game that the USGA guards its integrity in the face of commercial temptation. Because golf can be such a character-builder for young people, it will probably be studied in schools at all levels and, we can hope, socioeconomic layers.

Ultimately, as true gravity becomes widely accessible and universally practiced, golf will become a contest of club selection, green reading, and handling variables such as wind. There will be many Hogans, Palmers, and Nicklauses, and the masses will perform in the seventies and eighties instead of the nineties and hundreds. With attention to the three static positions and the other side of golf, the side which operates in true gravity, the game will finally, after many years of stagnation, truly evolve.

10

Putting and the Short Game

THE MYSTERY OF PUTTING! If there is anything more elusive than great putting, I can't
name it. The feel can come and go without
warning. Sometimes the line to the hole is as
vivid as if it were painted in broad strokes. And
sometimes the ball looks as if it can't possibly
fit into the whole. The mind can enlarge the
hole, or it can shrink it.

Positive thinking is a must when it comes to
putting. One of the best tips on putting that I
know involves a little visualization, and, with
practice, you can really make it work. If you
can imagine the hole being two feet wide, it
can really take the pressure off. Even if you
miss, you'll find yourself close enough for a
tap-in most of the time. Also, putting is so individualized that I believe that *the best way to
put is the way you putt best*.

I *can* give you one strategic tip that *will*
improve your putting, and I guarantee it will

work if you do it conscientiously and consistently: always play more than enough break and always reach the hole. With putting, you've just got to keep knocking on the door, coming close, and you'll make your share. But remember, you can make a perfect stroke along the perfect line to the hole and still miss if the ball encounters an imperfection or a small impediment on the putting surface and is knocked off course. But just keep coming close, that's the secret of putting.

Sometimes a beginner will ask me: "How do I know how hard to putt the ball?" I have them toss a ball to me from about twenty feet away and after they do, I ask, "How did you know how hard to toss it?" It is feel, it is instinct, and that, basically, is the secret to putting. That, and reading the green. When you putt, if you imagine that a ball is in your right hand (for righties), and you are rolling it to the hole with that hand, you'll be amazed at how accurate your distance judgment is when you rely on instinct. Remember, the putter is just an extension of your arms and is designed to transmit feel through the shaft to your hands.

One more thought on putting. You've heard the old saying "The more you practice, the luckier you get." Well, the more you practice, the more feel you'll have with the putter. Putting is the least practiced part of golf, and it should be just the opposite. I have given literally thousands of golf lessons, yet I can't recall a handful of people who have asked for a putting lesson. People just like to wallop the golf ball, but if you are serious about scoring lower, practice putting a lot more than you'd like to. It will pay off with increased feel, more putts that keep coming close, and therefore more putts that drop.

The Short Game

The short game is played from about fifty to sixty yards into the green and includes pitch-and-run shots, pitch shots, chips, and greenside bunker shots. These shots are much easier to learn than full shots for two very simple and logical reasons: the swing is shorter, and the distance of the shot is shorter. Using the three-static-positions method is very effective on these shots, especially the third position, the finish. Most players perform poorly around the greens because they use too long a backswing and not enough forward swing. In other words, they take the club back too far and decelerate on the forward swing.

There is a cardinal rule regarding shots *around* the green and *on* the green: *the follow-through should be equal to or greater than the backswing.* This guarantees acceleration—a vital element in effective shots on or near the green. Also, remember that whenever possible you want to try to land the ball on the putting surface and then let it roll to the flagstick. The green is much smoother than the surrounding areas and there will be decreased risk of crazy bounces.

My prescription for an effective short game is this: take a lesson or two on technique from a qualified PGA pro and then follow the above advice, paying particular attention to instinct and the three-static-positions method of practice. Your short game will improve dramatically, and so will your score. Remember, practice your short game more than you'd like to and more than you think you need to.

A strange effect takes place when your short game improves: your long game gets better. When the pressure to hit good shots all the time is lifted by your short-game confidence, your golf swing becomes freer, less tense, and thus more consistently effective.

Conclusion

IN ALL LIKELIHOOD, you probably have not experienced a great deal of significant improvement in your golf game, regardless of your handicap or how long you've been playing. I'm sure you've either taken lessons from a professional, studied numerous instructional books and/or articles, or both.

You may even have attended a golf school for several days of concentrated instruction. Typically, after any one of the above scenarios, your handicap has dropped a couple or three strokes. In most cases, this drop is due more to *increased* activity and *more* repetition than to any enlightening new information about the secrets of the game. On the more blatantly ludicrous side are the well-known newspaper ads promoting "special" balls and clubs that allow you to drive the ball forty to fifty yards farther. Research the handicap records at your club and compare the club roster's *average* handicap now with the same statistic five, ten, fifteen, twenty years ago. You'll quickly see that the golfing masses, as stated by the National Golf Foundation, have really improved very little, if at all, after all these years. Obviously, something is amiss, unless you want to believe that golf has some mysterious quality that makes it universally and permanently difficult. Most golfers have, quite simply, been focusing not just on mechanics, but on an area of mechanics that cannot be worked on to any influential degree. After many years in the same boat, I, after a series of unlikely events, and even some syncronicities of enormous impact, have developed, tested, and practiced methods that bring significant and accelerated results. The methods have been detailed in this book, and if you follow them with exacting diligence, they will improve your game dramatically and at the same time put you in touch with the real fiber of the art of golf. You will get to know your inner self, the part of you that always operates in true gravity, and you will learn not only how to coexist with your inner self but to exist *in conjunction* with it and tap into its strengths, purities, and unlimited capabilities. The lessons learned here can be a beacon of positive change for *all* of your life, not just golf. You will enjoy the game more and revel in its unique offerings.

What other activity of man can expose such a wide range of thought and action, such a cross-section of the human personality? It has been said that if you want to know all about a person, play eighteen holes with him and *walk* with him as you play. If you have any questions about Holographic Golf, or wish to discuss its application to you personally, feel free to contact me. So that the golfing masses will be able to learn these methods, I plan to institute a Holographic Golf research and training center, with qualified instructors trained in these methods.

There is more than one Shivas Irons out there, just waiting for the right catalyst.

Glossary

BALL FLINGING: A practice technique in which the golfer imagines that a magnetized golf ball clings to the club during the backswing and is released during the follow-through and flung toward the target. This encourages swinging through the ball rather than hitting at it with a wild swing.

BLENDING: A mental exercise in which negative course elements like wind, water hazards, and sand traps are turned into positive factors and "blended" into the swing.

EXPLICATE ORDER: The perceptible level of reality that we see in our daily lives. Our golf shots are in the explicate order. Also referred to as "unfolded."

FLAT PLANE: A horizontal swing plane.

HOLOGRAM: A three-dimensional image produced by a laser illuminating a piece of holographic film.

IMPLICATE ORDER: The imperceptible level of reality that gives birth to the objects and appearances of our physical world. Also referred to as "enfolded."

INTERCONNECTED: The idea that every part of a whole influences and is influenced by all other parts. For instance, proper preparation will affect the outcome of the golf shot.

POSITIVE LOCATION: The desired landing area for a golf shot, affording the easiest approach for the next shot. With positive visualization, the golfer pictures a very large positive location.

STATIC POSITION NUMBER ONE: The address position.

STATIC POSITION NUMBER TWO: The end of the backswing.

STATIC POSITION NUMBER THREE: The finish of the swing.

SWING ARC: The path the club head makes as it moves around the body.

SWING PLANE: The degree to which the swing arc is vertical or horizontal.

TEMPO: The rhythm and pace of a golf swing. Proper tempo is vital to a good swing.

TRUE GRAVITY: The deeper lines of force, the deeper structure of the universe. The "heart power" or "feeling force" that permeates all things. An awareness of "energy dimensions" and the relations of things.

UPRIGHT PLANE: A vertical swing plane.

THE ZONE: Purity of concentration, when negative thoughts are completely driven out by positive ones, enabling peak performance.